FOR FOOD'S SAKE

Recipes for use with a Thermomix

By Tenina Holder

COOKING WITH
TENINA

HUB & SPOKE
PUBLISHING

EVERY RECIPE TRIED AND PROVEN

To my dearest mum Jeanne, who always fed me well and always believed in me! XX

ABOUT TENINA

Food has long been at the core of Tenina Holder's life, encouraged from childhood by a mother whose own cooking was more adventurous than was usual for the time.

Born in the UK, Tenina came to Australia, to Melbourne, with her family when she was a toddler, returning to the UK for a period as a teenager before moving to Perth. She studied theatre arts at university in the US and it was there that her love of cooking began to emerge. She was the one who cooked for her grateful college mates on weekends, and how they appreciated her efforts. It was, she says, her relaxation, away from learning lines and studying.

Back home in Australia she found work as an actor in several popular food commercials. The result was a new interest in food, food styling and design, which she combined with motherhood – she has five children – and which took her on a different career path as a food consultant for Kleenmaid and later as head of recipe development at Thermomix in Australia.

She also began a food blog, long before it was fashionable, as a way of satisfying requests for her recipes. It's fair to say that, by then, she was hooked on thermal cooking as the way of her culinary future.

In this book - Tenina's first - she shares her stunning recipes, tips and photography. It's Australian-styled cooking, incorporating influences from her (well-known!) friends and global travels. A fresh, tried and proven approach - that will inspire and expand the boundaries of your cooking.

Find more of Tenina's recipes at www.tenina.com; join the conversation at www.facebook.com/cookingwithtenina; watch Tenina make her favourite recipes at www.youtube.com/teninastestkitchen

PRODUCTS I LOVE

I love the results that certain products bring to my food and I hope that you will seek out these products where possible!

HEILALA VANILLA

My absolute must-have in the pantry. You will find Heilala vanilla bean paste (VBP between friends) an incredible addition to any dessert. I am happy to endorse Heilala as the best ethical vanilla in the Asia Pacific region as well as the best in flavour. I sell it at my cooking classes.

You can find out about other Heilala products at **www.heilalavanilla.com** and perhaps you will join me on their annual foodie tour to the plantation in the near future.

CRIO BRÜ

Crio Brü is an all-cacao bean product that is roasted and ground like coffee and brewed into a drink, much the same as coffee but of course I am using it in everything I can. I find it to be the superfood it is claimed to be, and I love the results I have been having, such as lots of energy, feel-good euphoria (bring it on) and as an appetite suppressant. But most of all I just love the taste. With lots of variations from different exotic parts of the world to try, you will never be brewed out!

You can purchase Crio Brü online at **www.criobru.com.au**

LAUCKE FLOUR

Laucke Flour Mills was established in 1899. Since then, the Laucke family knowing that only "good grains make great flour", continue to produce flour and mixes for you to make healthy products at home with quality, reliability and flavour in mind.

www.laucke.com.au

WEIGH 'N PAY

I enjoy this family-run shop and their helpful, knowledgeable staff in Woodvale, W.A. They stock most ingredients that I use in my books, and you 'only pay for what you weigh'. They happily post it to all parts of Australia and are open Sundays.

www.weighnpay.com.au

GREEN & BLACK'S ORGANIC CHOCOLATE

I love chocolate (no surprises there!), but only the very best tasting chocolate. Green and Black's has always been a favorite in my kitchen - great for both eating and cooking. Chock full of organic ingredients, from bean to bar, you will not be disappointed. It can be easily found in most supermarkets, and is also stocked by health food and specialty stores. Do yourself a chocolate flavour.

COBRAM ESTATE EXTRA VIRGIN OLIVE OIL

Australia's most awarded extra virgin olive oil brand. On two large groves north of Melbourne, the company oversees production from seed to bottle. The onsite nursery, custom-built harvesting machines, advanced processing and storage technology, all help to ensure the highest levels of freshness and quality. Its bottles have a fantastic Pop-Up Pourer, and the range features 3 levels of intensity and various infused options.

www.cobramestate.com.au

YOUR PANTRY

The thing I love most about cooking with a TM is being able to make almost everything in it from go to whoa. And truly, my pantry has altered considerably because of using a TM. Your TM pantry should contain a few basics that you might spend a day here and there making. This allows you to keep cooking at your best, without having to take time out to make flavoured salts or butters, or mayonnaise. Designed to add maximum bang for your buck, these are my tried and true recipes that I use all the time. Many feature as ingredients in other recipes in the book. When I have a pantry (or fridge) full, I feel a deep sense of satisfaction. Perhaps I should just get out more!

If making this for the Curried Butternut Soup recipe, proceed to make soup without cleaning bowl.

YELLOW CURRY PASTE

Fragrant, aromatic, spicy curry paste…this is one you can use for so many things. We use it in the Curry Mayonnaise in this book as well as the Curried Butternut Soup, but if you wanted to use it for a simple chicken curry, just add onions, garlic, stock, chicken and coconut cream, steam the rice and it's all on!

NEED

- 8 dried red chillies
- 1 tsp cumin seeds
- 1 tsp coriander seeds
- Few cloves
- ½ stick cinnamon
- 1 tsp sea salt
- 1 stalk lemon grass, white part only
- Thumb-sized piece galangal, peeled
- 80g eschalots
- 2 cloves garlic
- 1 tbsp turmeric
- 50g oil

DO

1. Place chillies into small bowl and add enough boiling water to just cover.

2. Place cumin, coriander seeds, cloves and cinnamon into TM bowl and dry fry **11 min/Varoma/speed 1**. Cool slightly before milling **1 min/speed 9**.

3. Drain chillies. Place remaining ingredients into TM bowl and chop **2 sec/speed 6**. Scrape down sides of bowl. Sauté **8 min/Varoma/speed 2**. Blend **1 min/speed 6**. Scrape down sides of bowl and repeat blending if necessary.

4. Set aside until use or keep in sterilised jar in fridge until use. Will keep for up to 4 weeks.

UMAMI PASTE

Well kids, this is it! If you haven't already made this, I expect you to go no further until you have done so – it is a condition of buying my book! It is my game changer in the kitchen and I really can no longer cook without it. If you do a little research on Umami, it is the fifth taste, discovered in Japan in 1908 and described as a full-bodied meaty flavour with depth that is found in glutamate-rich foods. Some examples are mushrooms, seaweed, soy sauce, anchovies, blue cheese, parmesan and tomatoes. Of course there are many more. You can now add that touch of the irresistible to all your dishes with a little Umami Paste, your friend in the fridge.

NEED

- 300g roma tomatoes, cubed
- 90g parmesan, cubed
- 80g walnuts, toasted
- 5g Dulse sea vegetable flakes
- 5g good balsamic vinegar
- 2–3 anchovy fillets

DO

1. Place tomatoes into TM bowl and cook **10 min/100°C/Reverse + speed 1**.

2. Press cooled pulp through a fine sieve and separate solids from liquids. Reserve liquid to use in Umami Paste. See below for suggestion for tomato solids.

3. Place parmesan and walnuts into clean, dry TM bowl and mill **8 sec/speed 9**.

4. Add remaining ingredients and blend **30 sec/speed 4**, scraping down as necessary.

TASTE

- Serve on crostini, as is.
- Add to a cheese platter as a spread.
- Stir through hot soups, bolognaise sauce, curries, and any other savoury dishes as needed.
- Blend 1–2 tbsp Umami Paste through freshly made butter with some flat leaf parsley and lemon juice for a delicious U-Butter to top a grilled steak, fish, or as an alternative to garlic or herb butter.
- Add to risotto or stir through hot cooked pasta with chopped herbs and EVOO for a quick and easy meal.
- Rub onto uncooked chicken breast, wrap breast in sliced mozzarella and bacon and cook on hot grill.

TIP

- It is a little difficult to weigh the Dulse flakes, so divide the package that you purchase by guesswork.
- Dehydrate tomato solids in warm oven on a piece of baking paper for as long as it takes for it to become brittle. Mill and add to Chicken Stock Powder (see page 25).
- For a vegetarian option - omit anchovies and add 2 tbsp soy or tamari sauce.

You Tube
youtube.com/
teninastestkitchen

It's not rocket science but produces an amazing result. I love my flavoured salt collection. They add a zing of flavour to anything I, and occasionally my husband, cooks: 'Yes honey, just use the Citrus Olive Salt' or 'Try the Chilli Lime Salt on that chicken before you BBQ it'. Instant flavour.

FLAVOURED SALTS

NEED

- 100g good quality coarse salt
- Flavourings of choice

Vanilla Salt
- 1 vanilla bean (then follow directions below)

Chilli Lime Salt
- Zest 2–3 limes
- 2 chillies (dry zest and chillies in 130°C oven for 40–60 minutes, then follow directions below)

Citrus Olive Salt
- Zest 2 oranges
- Zest 1 lemon
- 50g Kalamata olives (dry zest and olives in 130°C oven for 40–60 minutes, then follow directions below)

Fennel Salt
- 2 tbsp fennel seeds, toasted (then follow directions below)

Saffron Salt
- Good pinch saffron threads (soak saffron in enough hot water to cover, drain, and then follow directions below)

DO

Coarse Grind

ⓘ Place salt and chosen prepared ingredients into TM bowl and blend **4–5 sec/Reverse + speed 6**.

Fine Grind

ⓘ Place salt and chosen prepared ingredients into TM bowl and blend **6 sec/speed 8**.

Note: Store in airtight jars, except Saffron Salt, which must be spread out onto a flat tray and left to 'dry' before putting into jars.

TASTE

- Use flavoured salts as rubs for uncooked meats, fish etc.
- Use as seasoning in place of regular salt on just about anything.
- Add Vanilla Salt to hot chocolate for a real treat.
- Tie your salt flavours to your cuisine.

- Vanilla Salt: Cajun or Caribbean
- Saffron Salt: Middle Eastern or Mediterranean
- Citrus Olive Salt: Mediterranean
- Fennel Salt: Mediterranean
- Chilli Lime Salt: Caribbean, South American or Asian

I am all about the flavour at the end of the day. So bring on flavoured butter, mayonnaise and salts. There is no limit to the flavours you can concoct with butter, as fat really carries the flavour of most things well. Knock yourself out with whatever flavours are the favourites in your household. The method for all is virtually the same, but occasionally you will have to add some blending time if you happen to have a stubborn piece of parmesan or herb sprig. If wrapped well, all these butters will keep in the freezer for around three months.

FLAVOURED BUTTERS

Try all of these in so many ways; As a spread on hot fresh rolls or bread, or cut a piece and allow to melt over grilled steak, chicken, or fish. Replace normal butter in a shortbread or pastry recipe for either a savoury or sweet addition to your recipe. Try over freshly steamed vegetables, on pancakes, to add something interesting to your ham or cheese sandwich, or just on crackers instead of a dip.

NEED

Bacon Herb Butter
- 200g unsalted butter, cubed
- Few leaves or pinch of dried oregano
- Freshly cracked black pepper
- 8 strips crisp crumbled bacon

Cumin Coriander Butter
- 200g unsalted butter, cubed
- 2 tsp ground cumin
- 2 tbsp coriander
- Pinch sea salt

Cheddar Butter
- 200g unsalted butter, cubed
- 200g Cheddar cheese, cubed
- ½ tsp Worcestershire sauce
- 1 clove garlic
- Pinch sea salt

Citrus Herb Butter
- 200g salted butter, cubed
- Juice ½ lemon
- Juice ½ orange
- Juice ½ lime
- Few tarragon leaves
- Few basil leaves
- Freshly ground black pepper
- ½ tsp sugar (optional)

Ginger Pecan Butter
- 200g unsalted butter, cubed
- 50g pecans, toasted
- 20g crystallised ginger
- 1 tbsp honey
- ½ tsp ground allspice

Olive Butter
- 200g unsalted butter, cubed
- 20g Kalamata or black olives, pitted
- Fresh lemon juice to taste

Hazelnut Butter
- 200g unsalted butter, cubed
- 60g hazelnuts, toasted
- 1 tsp honey

Onion Parmesan Butter
- 200g unsalted butter, cubed
- 30g parmesan cheese, cubed
- 2 spring onions/shallots, sliced

Blue Cheese Butter
- 200g unsalted butter, cubed
- 150g Blue Cheese, crumbled
- Few sprigs fresh parsley
- 30g brandy
- 2 cloves garlic
- Freshly ground black pepper to taste
- 1 tsp sweet chilli sauce

DO

Place all ingredients into TM bowl and blend **10 sec/speed 6**. Scrape down sides of bowl and repeat if necessary. Scrape onto a piece of baking paper, roll up into a sausage shape and refrigerate or freeze until use.

HAZELNUT CHOCOLATE SPREAD WITH SALTED CARAMEL DULCE DE LECHE

I am taking no prisoners with this one. If you are likely to become addicted to something, this may just be it. Make sure you have plans to give some away though – as it does make a lot. Perfect for gift-giving with style and class. I am pleased to say that this decadence was not entirely my idea, and having visited Darren at Burch & Purchese Sweet Studio in Melbourne, it wasn't long before I was plotting my own version of their delicious concoction; so thanks for the memories guys!

HAZELNUT SPREAD

NEED

- 100g hazelnuts, roasted and skinned
- 50g sugar
- 100g milk
- 100g dark chocolate, in pieces
- 100g unsalted butter, cubed
- 2 tbsp cocoa
- 1 tsp vanilla extract

DO

1. Place nuts and sugar into TM bowl and mill **10 sec/ speed 10**.

2. Add remaining ingredients and cook **8 min/60°C/ speed 3**.

3. Half fill sterilised jars and set aside to cool and set completely.

DULCE DE LECHE

NEED

- 800g full cream milk
- 250g brown sugar
- 1 tsp vanilla bean paste
- 50g golden syrup
- 1 tsp coarse sea salt

DO

1. Place milk, sugar, and vanilla bean paste into TM bowl and cook **8 min/90°C/speed 4**.

2. Add golden syrup and salt. Cook **30 min/Varoma/ speed 4**. Place basket on top of lid to allow reduction with minimum mess.

3. Blend **30 sec/speed 6**. Pour on top of set Hazelnut Spread and cool before keeping in refrigerator until use.

TASTE

- Jars of this would make a beautiful gift with small tags and ribbons. Serve with brioche toast, croissants, or melt a little for a topping on ice-cream or crepes.

DRIED APRICOT PRESERVES

Somehow 'preserves' sounds a little more homely than ordinary old 'jam'. A little more 'grandma in the kitchen cooking up a batch of fragrant fruit', don't you think? I have always loved fresh apricots but clearly they are not available for most of the year in Australia. You can, however, get good dried apricots year round and they will make the most excellent apricot 'preserves'. I have yet to try other dried fruits, but stay tuned, that task is on my 'Reserve for Preserves' list!

NEED

- 400g dried Australian apricots
- 350g water
- 250g sugar
- 100g lemon juice, fresh

DO

1. Place apricots and water into TM bowl and cook **10 min/100°C/Reverse + speed 1**.

2. Add remaining ingredients and cook **20 min/90°C Reverse + speed 1**.

3. Pour into hot sterilised jars and cool. Try not to eat it all on the first sitting. If you would like it a little less thick, add extra lemon juice after cooking and testing the set. But then cook it for a further 5 minutes.

CITRUS CURD

Lemon Curd or Butter has long been a favourite in my household, so much so that I often whip up a batch for breakfast as I am cooking the crepes. (Bless you, TM.) This is just my version – you can use any citrus juice, all-lime is sensational and pink grapefruit is also pretty fantastic.

NEED

- 220g sugar
- Zest 1 lemon
- Zest 1 lime
- 240g unsalted butter, cubed
- 200g mixed citrus juice
- 4 eggs + 2 egg yolks

DO

1. Place sugar with zests into TM bowl and mill **10 sec/speed 10**.

2. Add butter and chop **5 sec/speed 7**.

3. Add remaining ingredients. Cook **10 min/80°C/speed 6**.

4. Cook **2 min/90°C/speed 6**.

5. Pour into sterilised jars and seal.

TASTE

- This makes a great tart filling – make a quick vanilla bean pastry, blind bake mini tartlets, and just before serving, dollop in cold citrus curd.
- Stir curd through whipped cream, add fresh raspberries and cubes of sponge cake for a quick dessert.
- Serve over vanilla ice-cream as an elegant topping and it is fantastic on brioche toast, French toast or even brioche French toast....can you imagine?

VA VOOM VANILLA AND STRAWBERRY JAM

I love the fragrance of strawberry jam cooking any time, but add the vanilla bean and it pushes it up to heavenly. Everyone will want to taste this, piping hot or not, as the heady aroma fills your kitchen. But be warned. It is hotter than the sun when it has just been cooked. Ok?

NEED

- 400g strawberries (fresh or frozen)
- 200g caster sugar
- 1 green apple, quartered, skin on
- 1 vanilla bean, cut into pieces

DO

1. Place all ingredients into TM bowl and cook **35 min/ Varoma/speed 1** with simmering basket on top of lid in place of the MC.

2. Check the consistency of the jam by placing a spoonful onto a cold plate. If it wrinkles up when pushed, the jam is ready. If not, cook **10 min/ Varoma/speed 1** at a time and check after each time period, up to 30 minutes more, until it has reached the consistency that you like.

TASTE

- Dollop on everything; scones, fresh bread or brioche, pancakes, French toast, doughnuts, sponge cake… and, of course, with the obligatory mounds of freshly whipped cream.

BERRY LIME COULIS

This is a simple dessert sauce that you can easily vary to your own taste. Great with most desserts, excellent on ice-cream and well used in the recipes of this book. Freeze it in cubes for easy storage.

NEED

- 300g red berries of choice, fresh or frozen
- 65g sugar
- Zest 1 lime, finely grated
- Juice 1 lime

DO

1. Place all ingredients into TM bowl and cook **8 min/90°C/speed 1**.

2. Blend **1 min/speed 6**.

3. Strain through fine mesh sieve and pour into sterilised glass jar. Refrigerate until use.

TIP

- This recipe can be doubled easily, just add 2 minutes to the cooking time. It will keep for up to 3 weeks in the fridge and indefinitely in the freezer.

HERBED HOLLANDAISE

Notoriously difficult to make (without a TM), hollandaise is delicious for Eggs Benedict or Florentine, over asparagus, on steamed vegies, as part of a filling in pancakes or, just quietly, out of the pot with a spoon. Whoever thought of beating butter into a delicate mixture of herbs and tangy reduction was a genius.

NEED

Reduction
- 10 peppercorns
- 100g white wine vinegar
- 100g verjuice
- Handful herbs of choice

Hollandaise
- 1 egg

- 2 egg yolks
- 20g reduction liquid
- Pinch sea salt
- 1 tsp lemon juice, fresh
- 200g unsalted butter, melted

DO

1. Place all reduction ingredients into a heavy-based saucepan and simmer on a medium heat (Induction 6) until reduced by at least half. Strain.

2. To make hollandaise insert Butterfly into TM bowl and add egg, egg yolks, reduction, salt and lemon juice. Whip **10 min/80°C/speed 3**.

3. Increase temperature and whip **2 min/90°C/speed 3**.

4. Drizzle butter through hole in lid and incorporate **3 min/speed 3**.

5. Serve immediately.

TIP

- You must remove the finished hollandaise from the TM bowl as soon as it is done or the residual heat will continue to cook the sauce and it will curdle or scramble.

GOURMET MAYOS

Apparently there is a store in NYC that has just opened up selling only mayonnaise. While I think that is a little too exclusive, I understand the passion about mayonnaise. The things you can add to mayo to take it above and beyond this world are wide and varied, so get ready for the new taste sensations that are specified here. Your mission, if you choose to accept it, is to never more fail at mayonnaise, and to forever more add flavour above and beyond the call of duty.

CURRY MAYONNAISE

NEED

- 2 egg yolks
- 15g white wine vinegar
- 1 tsp Dijon mustard
- 30g Yellow Curry Paste (see page 7)
- Pinch sea salt
- 400g grapeseed oil
- Juice 2 limes

DO

1. Place egg yolks, vinegar, mustard, curry paste and salt into TM bowl and mix **1 min/37°C/speed 5**.

2. Gradually add oil through hole in lid with MC in place, **4 min/speed 5**.

3. Add lime juice and blend **10 sec/speed 5**. Scrape into sterilised jar and keep in fridge up to 3 weeks.

TASTE

- Fantastic with chicken or egg salad, on sandwiches, pita bread etc. Also great with seafood or potato salad.

WASABI & LIME MAYONNAISE

NEED

- 2 egg yolks
- 15g white wine vinegar
- 20g wasabi paste (more or less to taste)
- Pinch sea salt
- 400g grapeseed oil
- Juice 2 limes

DO

1. Place egg yolks, vinegar, wasabi paste and salt into TM bowl and mix **1 min/37°C/speed 5**.

2. Gradually add oil through hole in lid with MC in place, **4 min/speed 5**.

3. Add lime juice and blend **10 sec/speed 5**. Scrape into sterilised jar and keep in fridge up to 3 weeks.

TASTE

- Delicious on steamed fish, as the dressing in sushi, on a rice and tuna salad. Divine in a tuna dip.

SUNDRIED TOMATO MAYONNAISE

NEED

- 30g semi sundried tomatoes
- 2 egg yolks
- 15g white wine vinegar
- 1 tsp Dijon mustard
- Pinch sea salt
- 400g grapeseed oil
- Juice 1 lemon

DO

1. Place tomatoes into TM bowl and chop for **5 sec/speed 6**. Scrape down sides of bowl and add egg yolks, vinegar, mustard and salt into TM bowl and mix **1 min/37°C/speed 5**.

2. Gradually add oil through hole in lid with MC in place, **4 min/speed 5**.

3. Add lemon juice and blend **10 sec/speed 5**. Scrape into sterilised jar and keep in fridge up to 3 weeks.

TASTE

- Use like any other mayonnaise, but especially good with seafood, tossed through hot cooked pasta or on sandwiches, or again, potato salad.

BACONNAISE

NEED

- 200g rendered bacon fat (discussed below)
- 30g crispy bacon pieces left over from the rendering
- 2 egg yolks
- 15g white wine vinegar
- 1 tsp Dijon mustard
- Cracked black pepper to taste
- Grapeseed oil as needed
- Juice ½ lemon or to taste

DO

1. Render the bacon fat by placing speck, streaky or relatively fatty bacon (500g approx.) in low heat frypan (Induction 4–5) and allow fat to 'render'. Set fat aside and allow to cool without solidifying. The fat MUST BE COOL, not set.

2. Place bacon pieces into TM bowl and chop **4 sec/speed 5**.

3. Add egg yolks, vinegar, mustard and pepper to TM bowl and mix **1 min/37°C/speed 5**.

4. Add bacon fat very slowly through hole in lid with MC in place, **4 min/speed 5**.

5. Add extra oil to make up volume if needed. (You can generally add up to 500g fat to 2 egg yolks as a ratio guide.)

6. Scrape down lid and sides of bowl and add lemon juice. Blend **10 sec/speed 5**. Scrape into sterilised jar and keep in fridge up to 3 weeks.

TASTE

- Use as you would any mayonnaise, but try it with sweet potato oven fries, on a steak, or in a burger, sandwich or as potato salad dressing.

CRANBERRY AND ALMOND GRANUESLI

I wasn't going to put this in the book, but you guys asked (no, begged) for it, so here it is! Our favourite idea using this is as a breakfast parfait: layers of granuesli, natural yoghurt, and stewed or fresh fruit of choice. Absolutely fantastic. I could open up a B & B with this recipe alone!

NEED

- 150g unsalted butter, cubed
- 150ml maple syrup or honey
- Good pinch sea salt
- 2 tbsp vanilla bean paste
- 300g whole almonds
- 60g sunflower seeds
- 4–5 cups rolled oats
- 100g craisins (dried cranberries)
- 50g shredded coconut

DO

1. Place butter, syrup, salt and vanilla into TM bowl and melt **4 min/60°C/speed 2**. Remove from bowl and set aside.

2. Meanwhile, spread nuts and seeds onto large flat tray and toast in 200°C oven (no need to preheat) for about 10 minutes until crunchy. Set aside to cool slightly.

3. Spread oats onto tray and drizzle with butter mixture. Stir and mix by hand until evenly distributed. Reduce oven temperature to 160°C. Cook oats 20 minutes, stirring occasionally to ensure edges are not overdone. If not fragrant and crispy enough, cook a further 5–10 minutes. (This will depend on your oven.)

4. Place cooled nuts into TM bowl and chop roughly **3 sec/speed 4**. Place into large mixing bowl. Cool oats slightly before adding to the bowl.

5. Add craisins and coconut and mix by hand. Allow to cool completely before storing in an airtight container for up to 4 weeks...but it won't last that long, I can assure you!

TASTE

- Try adding a handful of toasted pecans, choc chips, dried cherries, chopped dried apricots, goji berries, Crio Brü granules, other seeds or fruit of choice.

This is both a salute
and a return to convenience. I love being
able to grab a tablespoon or two of this,
add it to water in lots of recipes, without
losing any flavour and without starting
from the VERY beginning — killing
the chook, to make the stock, to make the
chicken soup, to make the pot pie, to, well,
you get the message. The cost savings on
liquid stock and more importantly, my time,
are significant. Enjoy.

CHICKEN STOCK POWDER

NEED

- Skin and carcass of 1 roasted chicken
- 2–3 sticks celery including leaves
- 2 carrots, peeled and sliced
- 1 onion, quartered with layers split
- 100g dried onion flakes
- 20g celery seed
- 40g dried mushrooms
- 40g dehydrated peas
- 100g Celtic sea salt

DO

1. Preheat oven to 160°C and line a large baking tray with baking paper.

2. Spread chicken skin, break up carcass and spread across paper.

3. Add fresh vegetables in a single layer if possible. Bake for 40 minutes, then reduce heat to 140°C and leave in oven until all vegetables are dried out. (You can use a dehydrator for this process if desired.)

4. Remove as much flesh from the carcass as possible. Discard bones. Place all dried chicken, skin and all (dried & dehydrated) vegetables into TM. Blend **1 min/speed 9**.

5. Add remaining ingredients and blend **20 sec/speed 10**.

6. Keep refrigerated and use in place of stock cubes at a ratio of 1 tbsp = 1 stock cube or as directed in recipes in this book.

7. This should keep indefinitely in the fridge due to the high salt content.

ROSEMARY AND FENNEL APPLE SAUCE

Pass the pork crackle and no one will get hurt – that's the catchcry at my house when pork is on its way out of the oven. This sauce is the perfect accompaniment to a roasted pork and its crackle. Try it with baked ham as well.

NEED

- 200g apples, cored and peeled
- 30g sugar
- 1 sprig rosemary, leaves only
- ½ tsp fennel seeds
- Pinch sea salt
- 20g white wine
- 70g water

DO

1. Place apples, sugar, rosemary, fennel seeds and salt into TM bowl and chop **4 sec/speed 4**.

2. Add wine and water and cook **15 min/100°C/speed 1**.

3. Serve with roasted pork.

POWDERED MALT

I learnt this little trick on my last visit to Europe in the lovely test kitchen of my friend in Germany. I cannot tell you what a difference it has made to my baked goods. I make sure I have a jar of malt in my pantry at all times and so should you. It will show up in more and more of my recipes in the future, so now is the time to get it organised and into your pantry.

NEED

- 200g whole wheat
- Tepid water as needed
- Steamer tray, colander or tray with holes

DO

1. Sprout wheat over a period of days by rinsing in warm water, and draining through colander. Rinse about 2–3 times a day to keep grains moist, but not soggy.

2. Keep grains in the colander on a plate, and spread them around so that they are separated. Sunshine will speed up the process.

3. When you have 'decent' sprouts (½cm in length) place onto a flat baking tray and spread out into single layer. Allow to dry for a few hours.

4. Place into preheated 160°C oven and roast for 25–30 minutes until sprouts are fragrant and golden. They should be crunchy and edible at this stage.

5. Place cooled sprouts into TM bowl and mill for **1 min/ speed 9**. Store in airtight jar and use as desired.

TASTE

- Use 1–2 tbsp in all baked goods for a distinctive sweet taste and a browner, glossy appearance.
- Adding malt to your breads eliminates the need for sugar to feed the yeast, will help achieve a higher rise and give you a browner, more fragrant crust.

EASY BEGINNINGS

The best thing about having my family around for a meal is not just that I get them there with the lure of great food – it's also the standing around the kitchen having a chat while I finish preparations. To go with that casual time, a few nibbles or 'something' to be getting on with is important. I think the same is true with friends, and so here are a few of my favourite crowd pleasers. You can choose to be more formal or just use these dishes as a teaser for the good stuff to come!

CARAMELISED GARLIC PASTE

NEED

- 3 whole heads garlic
- 25g balsamic vinegar
- 30g EVOO
- 2 tbsp dark brown sugar
- Generous pinch sea salt

DO

1. Place garlic heads and enough water to cover them into TM bowl and cook **10 min/Varoma/Reverse + speed 1**. Drain garlic through simmering basket and cool slightly before cutting through whole heads and squeezing out soft garlic cloves from skins.

2. Return garlic flesh to the clean, dry TM bowl and add vinegar, EVOO, sugar and salt.

3. Cook **8 min/Varoma/Reverse + speed 1**. Cool slightly before blending, for a coarse texture, **5 sec/speed 4** or for a smooth result, **5 sec/speed 6** or until desired consistency is reached. Keep in sterilised jar in the fridge until use.

TASTE

- While delicious on its own, try using a dollop in sauces for an instant flavour lift. Spread on toast or crostini, chicken or steak before grilling. Spread on a pastry base for quiche before adding the filling…you get the idea. It will keep in the fridge for up to a month.

If you follow me on Tenina.com you will know that just about every other recipe has a pesto involved. They are quick and wonderful ways to add a punch to salad dressings, tart or sandwich fillings, roasted vegies, or simply with crackers or crudités at a moment's notice. While the traditional basil, pine nut, parmesan combo is always divine, I thought it was time to shake the tree and see what other combos fell out. I loved all of these.

WALNUT PESTO

NEED

- 100g parmesan cheese, cubed
- 30g bottled red peppers
- Handful basil leaves
- 40g walnuts, toasted
- 2 cloves garlic
- 50g EVOO
- Sea salt and freshly cracked black pepper to taste

DO

1. Place cheese into TM bowl and mill **10 sec/speed 9**.

2. Add remaining ingredients and blend **10 sec/speed 6**. Scrape down and repeat if necessary.

TASTE

- Use as a dip, on crostini or toasted Turkish bread.
- Try adding double the EVOO and then drizzle over grilled prawns or chicken.
- Toss through hot pasta or use in place of pizza sauce before adding toppings as usual.
- Several other recipes in this book suggest 'pesto of choice'…so choose it!

SUNDRIED TOMATO PESTO

NEED

- 1 sprig rosemary, foliage only
- 4 cloves garlic
- 30g semi sundried tomatoes
- 60g Kalamata olives, pitted
- 2 tsp sugar
- 2 tsp balsamic vinegar
- 100g blanched almonds, toasted
- 100g EVOO
- 1 tsp smoked paprika
- Sea salt and freshly cracked black pepper

DO

1. Place rosemary, garlic, tomatoes and olives into TM bowl and chop **5 sec/speed 5**. Scrape down sides of bowl.

2. Add remaining ingredients and blend **6 sec/speed 6**. Scrape down sides of bowl and repeat if necessary.

PEA PUREE CROSTINI

This is a fresh, pretty and tasty start to any meal, or use it for a simple lunch with a salad and good friends…Such a quick one, that you can really do this as your guests arrive. (But do pre-make the baguette!)

NEED

- 150g frozen peas
- 35g cream
- 35g unsalted butter, cubed
- 12–14 slices French Baguette (see page 44)
- EVOO as needed
- 1 clove garlic
- Sliced cheeses of choice (a creamy blue is good)
- Few herb sprigs of choice (thyme is good)

DO

1. Place peas, cream and butter into TM bowl and cook **5 min/100°C/speed 2**. Puree **15 sec/speed 7**. Cool slightly.

2. Meanwhile brush each slice of bread with EVOO and heat a grill pan on high. Toast each side of bread and rub with garlic.

3. Top with puree, cheese and herbs to serve. Serve warm.

TASTE

- If you use a salty cheese do not add salt to the puree. If using a creamy cheese (like ricotta) you may need to adjust seasoning in puree to taste. Asiago, taleggio or camembert are wonderful choices with this recipe.

SWISS CHEESE AND HAM PASTRIES

12 PIECES

You know by now that I LOVE all Swiss food. In particular, I find a great Swiss cheese is hard to pass by. I made this recipe when I returned from my first trip to Zurich. I was in love with the countryside, the beauty of the architecture, the culture, the macarons, and yes, the Swiss cheese, particularly raclette. But as it costs more in Australia, go ahead and use Jarlsberg or, at a pinch, Dutch maasdam, which will lend this recipe the little sweetness it needs.

NEED

- 3 sheets commercial butter puff pastry, thawed OR 1 recipe Flaky Butter Pastry (see page 54), divided and rolled into 3 large squares
- 1 large egg + 1 egg yolk
- 120g crème fraiche (or sour cream)

- 40g unsalted butter
- 30g corn flour
- 120g whole milk
- Sea salt and freshly ground black pepper to taste

- Jarlsberg or gruyere cheese (or go wild and use raclette), thinly sliced
- Black Forest ham, thinly sliced
- Egg wash

DO

1. Preheat oven to 200°C. Line 2 baking trays with paper.

2. Cut puff pastry sheets in half and set aside.

3. Make béchamel sauce by placing egg and egg yolk, crème fraiche, butter, corn flour and milk into TM bowl and cook **6 min/100°C/speed 4**. Cool.

4. Lay cheese and ham slices across 1 half of each pastry sheet leaving room around the edges to seal. Top with béchamel and cover with other half of pastry. Seal borders with a fork or small knife. Slash tops to allow steam to escape and brush liberally with egg wash. Bake for 20–25 minutes until puffed and golden. Serve hot.

SMOKED SALMON CREPE TORTE

SERVINGS 8–10

It must be in my blood, but I love smoked salmon and crepes, and bagels and pasta … Add a little Herbed Hollandaise and you are in entrée heaven. This is very impressive as a dinner party starter, easily made ahead, and leftovers are sensational. If there are any.

NEED

Pancakes
- 2–3 spring onions/shallots, sliced
- 1 sprig fresh dill
- 2 eggs
- 400g milk
- 200g plain flour

- Sea salt
- EVOO for frying

Filling
- Handful herbs of choice
- 20g capers
- 250g cream cheese

- 100g celery, chopped
- 40g lemon juice, fresh
- 100g smoked salmon

DO

① Make pancakes by placing all ingredients into TM bowl and blend **30 sec/speed 8**.

② Rest batter for at least 10 minutes before cooking pancakes one at a time in an oiled frypan set to a medium heat (Induction 7). Set pancakes aside to cool.

③ Line the base of a springform cake tin with baking paper. Try and pick a tin that is approx. the same diameter as the frypan you use to make the pancakes.

④ To make filling, place all ingredients except salmon into TM bowl and blend **6 sec/speed 6**. Add salmon and blend **3 sec/speed 6**.

⑤ Lay 1 pancake into base of prepared tin. Spread with filling, cover with another pancake, repeat with filling and so on until all filling is used. Finish with a pancake. Press down and place into fridge for 1 hour.

⑥ Remove from tin, garnish with additional dill sprigs and grape tomatoes. Serve in wedges with salad or in thin slivers as a starter.

TASTE

- Not essential, but please feel free to add lashings of Herbed Hollandaise.

This recipe is like the little black dress, understated, almost plain, but stunning in its simplicity. It will have you invited to parties all over the country, as long as you promise to bring it. But be warned — the little black dress won't fit you much longer if you make it too often.

CAMEMBERT EN CROÛTE

NEED

- 1 eschalot (25g approx.)
- 100g Swiss brown mushrooms
- 10g EVOO
- 15g Umami Paste (see page 9)
- 1 heaped tsp corn flour
- 20g dry sherry
- 250g–1kg wheel of Camembert
- ½ qty Flaky Butter Pastry (see page 54) (make ahead) OR 1–2 sheets commercial puff pastry
- Egg wash

DO

1. Place eschalot, mushrooms, EVOO, Umami Paste, corn flour and dry sherry into TM bowl and chop **3 sec/speed 5**.

2. Sauté **10 min/100°C/speed 1**, with MC off. Remove from bowl and cool completely.

3. Preheat oven to bread setting 180°C and line a flat tray with baking paper.

4. Roll out pastry into a large round sheet. Spread cold mushroom mixture into the centre, approx. the circumference of your cheese.

5. Place the cheese on top and carefully wrap, sealing edges well. Turn over and lay, seam side down, on prepared tray. Decorate with leftover pastry if desired. Brush with egg wash and bake for 30 minutes or until golden brown.

6. Serve immediately with plates…this is fantastic for a crowd if you use a large wheel of cheese, simply supply napkins and small cheese knives and let them at it!

TASTE

- A great do-it-ahead recipe. Make the entire thing, without baking; simply wrap and freeze until ready to bake. Put straight into preheated oven from the freezer and add 15 minutes baking time to allow for thawing.

SAVOURY POTTED CHEESE

It's probably because of my time spent in the US, but anything that adds butter to cheese can't be bad, can it? Make this and get back to me on that...

NEED

- 100g parmesan, cubed
- 200g vintage cheddar, cubed
- 35g unsalted butter, cubed
- 1 tsp mustard powder
- 40g dry sherry
- 30g red onion
- 1 clove garlic

DO

1. Place cheeses into TM bowl and mill **10 sec/speed 9**.

2. Add remaining ingredients and blend **1 min/speed 6**. Scrape down sides of bowl and repeat if necessary.

3. Pot into sterilised jars and seal until use. Keep refrigerated.

TASTE

- Serve in the jar as part of a cheese board, or use in place of mayonnaise on a baguette with salad, tuna, ham or sliced meat of choice.

BREADS

Here is a limited collection of my absolute yeasty favourites. With the amazing ability to warm and stir in the TM, you must try fresh yeast. Dried yeast will work in all of these recipes, however. If you were ever afraid of fresh yeast in the past, forget your fears. You just need to find a yeast supplier and voilà, you will be channelling your inner baker in no time.

To add wet items to a bread dough, dredge them in flour first, eg if adding Kalamata olives and toasted walnuts to your bread (pictured) toss them through about 2 tbsp flour. Hand knead them in after the first rise and before forming the loaf. Dust the formed loaf with lots of flour and do not steam prior to baking in the hottest oven you can achieve. A pizza stone is ideal. Increase baking time as needed.

The flavour and aroma of sourdough is hard to beat. But the process of growing and maintaining the starter can be too much for a busy person. This easy version is not really a sourdough, but it will develop the right flavour the longer you keep and re-use your starter. It has had rave reviews, so please give it a go.

'CHEATS' SOURDOUGH

MAKES 2 LOAVES

NEED

- 30g fresh yeast
- 1 tsp sugar
- 300g water
- Pinch salt

- 550g bakers flour
- 2 tbsp Powdered Malt (see page 26) (optional)
- 20g EVOO

- (200g starter)
- 1L water for steaming

DO

1. Place yeast, sugar, water and salt into TM bowl and warm **2 min/37°C/speed 2**.

2. Add remaining ingredients and mix **10 sec/speed 6**.

3. Knead **2 min/Interval**.

4. Turn out onto Silpat mat and punch into tight ball. Wrap tightly and allow to double. Reserve 200g dough in plastic bag and set aside. (This is your new starter.)

5. Punch down dough and shape into 2 loaves. Place each loaf onto a separate sheet of baking paper.

6. Preheat oven to 220°C and heat pizza stone if possible.

7. Place water into TM bowl and bring to the boil **8 min/Varoma/speed 2**.

8. Place one loaf into steamer dish and cook **10 min/Varoma/speed 3**.

9. Remove bread and slide onto pizza stone immediately. Bake for 8 minutes. Repeat with remaining loaf.

TIP

- The very first loaf you make will have no starter. Proceed as directed without the starter.
- Keep your starter in the fridge and bring it out to warm it up every day between loaves. You simply add the starter to each loaf you make, reserve 200g of the new dough for the next loaf. You will find over time it will increase in 'sour' flavour and become very sticky. The more often you make bread, the better the flavour becomes. Make sure you use the starter as often as possible. It needs to be at room temperature before adding to a new dough.
- If you wish to use the starter as your rising agent, it is possible, but the rising time will be significantly longer. You will get an amazing crumb, a more sour flavour and it is well worth the time.
- Use wholegrain flours, rye is particularly good for sourness.
- Add olives, sundried tomatoes, rosemary, garlic, cheese, spinach, and so on, to your loaves as you would any other dough.

I was never interested in science at school but I am now fascinated by the science of all things food such as: Why use buttermilk instead of normal milk in these rolls? Essentially, the acid in the buttermilk breaks down the gluten in the flour and you have these amazingly Soft Buttermilk Rolls. (Go find a recipe for one of the Flavoured Butters in this book – I will not be held responsible though for your lack of self-control!)

SOFT BUTTERMILK ROLLS

16 ROLLS

NEED

Roux
- 30g flour
- 30g sugar
- 120g buttermilk

Dough
- 350g bakers flour
- Good pinch salt
- 20g unsalted butter, cubed
- 210g buttermilk
- 7g sachet dried instant yeast

DO

1. Place Roux ingredients into TM bowl and cook **3 min/80°C/speed 3**. Cool slightly. Leave in TM bowl.

2. Add all dough ingredients except yeast to cooked Roux in TM bowl and mix **10 sec/speed 6**. Add yeast and knead **4 min/Interval**. Scrape out onto floured Silpat mat and wrap in a tight ball. Prove until doubled.

3. Shape into rolls with wet hands. (This makes the stickiness easier to cope with.) Place on paper lined baking tray, cover and rise until doubled. Place into cold oven and bake for 15–20 minutes at 180°C.

4. Serve hot.

SWEET BUTTER GLAZED ROLLS

16 ROLLS

NEED

- 30g fresh yeast
- 55g water
- 70g sugar
- 55g unsalted butter, cubed
- 1 tsp salt
- 220g buttermilk or milk
- 1 egg
- 680g bakers flour
- Melted butter to brush rolls

DO

1. Place yeast, water, sugar, butter, salt and milk into TM bowl and warm **2 min/37°C/speed 2**.

2. Add egg and flour and mix **10 sec/speed 6**.

3. Knead **2 min/Interval**.

4. Turn out onto floured Silpat mat and bring dough together into tight ball. Wrap and prove until doubled.

5. Form into rolls and place on paper-lined baking tray. Brush with melted butter and allow to double again before baking in 200°C oven for 12–15 minutes or until lightly golden.

TIP

- Using a cold oven produces another little rise for your dough.

FRENCH BAGUETTE

MAKES 1

═══ NEED ═══

- 20g fresh yeast
- 180g warm water
- 370g bakers flour
- 1 tsp sea salt
- 1L water for steaming

═══ DO ═══

1. Place water and yeast into TM bowl and warm **2 min/37°C/speed 2**.

2. Add flour and salt and blend **15 sec/speed 6–7**.

3. Knead **3 min/Interval** speed. Allow to 'rest' for 5–10 minutes. (Go shower, water the garden, plan the toppings for this most delish bread, put on your make up!) Knead again **2 min/Interval speed**.

4. Turn out into oiled bowl and cover completely with plastic wrap so the air will be trapped and allow to double. The dough will be quite hard and dense, yet flexible.

5. When happy with the rise, punch down and roll into a flat rectangular shape. Fold both long sides towards each other. Tuck in the ends and seal together by pinching dough together.

6. Turn over so that the seam is down and you have a nice smooth top. Place onto baking paper and allow to rise again. Cover with floured tea towel.

7. Preheat pizza stone in a 220°C oven.

8. Pour water into TM bowl and heat **8 min/Varoma/speed 3**.

9. When ready to cook, cut several slashes across the dough. Leaving the loaf on the baking paper, place into steamer dish and set into position. Steam **10 min/100°C/speed 3**.

10. Transfer to hot oven and cook for a further 10–15 minutes. Loaf should sound hollow when tapped. Slice and try not to eat in one sitting.

It was bound to happen. The perfect loaf – chewy crust, full flavour, strong texture and great crumb. In France, laws prohibit the use of preservatives in bread production so baking baguettes is a daily task. With this recipe it can be a daily occurrence in your house, too. And you can double the ingredients (the method remains the same).

To make normal brioche, follow the same method, simply omit the chocolate and dried cherries.

CHOCOLATE CHERRY BRIOCHE

8 INDIVIDUAL BRIOCHE

I have to admit that until I visited Paris and tried real French brioche, I had only ever been deeply disappointed by it. When I started to bake my own, a whole new world in butter and yeast-related yumminess was opened up to me. In a good brioche, the cold butter remains in little granules in the dough and you get a bite of buttery goodness with every mouthful, so be sure to use a good butter – lash out and buy a beautiful, cultured European or Australian butter. It will be a flavour revelation.

NEED

- 150g unsalted butter, cubed
- 2 eggs
- 30g fresh yeast
- 60g sugar
- 130g milk

- 400g bakers flour
- 1 tsp salt
- 50g dark chocolate, in pieces
- 50g dried cherries

DO

1. Place cubed butter on plate in freezer.

2. Place eggs, yeast, sugar and milk into TM bowl and blend **10 sec/speed 5**. Warm **2 min/37°C/speed 1**.

3. Add flour, salt and knead **3 min/Interval**. Through hole in lid, add cubed butter a little at a time. The finished dough will be sticky and glossy, but quite malleable. Add chocolate and dried cherries right at the end of the kneading process for a few seconds, just to incorporate without breaking them up.

4. Scrape out onto floured Silpat mat and, with buttered hands, knead into a smooth ball. Do not be tempted to add flour.

5. Place into buttered glass bowl, cover tightly with plastic wrap and place in fridge overnight (or for at least 12 hours) to rise slowly.

6. Punch down and place into bread or brioche tin. Allow to rise in a 40°C oven for as long as it takes to double. (It may take a couple of hours as the dough has to 'wake up' after being in the fridge.)

7. Brush with egg wash before baking for 15–20 minutes in 200°C oven on a bread setting until sounding hollow when tapped on the bottom. Remove from tin and place back in the turned-off oven to dry the crust a little.

CINNAMON SCROLLS WITH CREAM CHEESE FROSTING

20 SCROLLS

I lived in the US for quite a few years and I must give the Americans this: they know how to do baked goods to die for. This is my attempt at recreating the famous Cinnabon bun, the aroma of which is enough to drive a sane dieter completely insane.

NEED

Dough
- 20g fresh yeast
- 2 eggs
- 60g unsalted butter, cubed
- 250g milk
- 80g sugar
- Pinch sea salt
- 650g bakers flour

Filling
- 1 dried vanilla bean (see across)
- 1 cinnamon stick
- 140g dark brown sugar
- 50–60g unsalted butter, cubed, room temperature

Frosting
- 100g cream cheese
- 2 tsp vanilla bean paste
- 100g icing sugar
- 50g unsalted butter, cubed

DO

1. Place yeast, eggs, butter, milk and 1 tsp of the sugar into TM bowl and warm **2 min/37°C/speed 2**. Add remaining dough ingredients and mix **10 sec/speed 6**.

2. Knead **3 min/Interval**. Knead by hand into a tight ball and wrap in Silpat mat until doubled in size. Butter a large rectangular baking dish and set aside.

3. To make filling, place cinnamon stick, vanilla bean and sugar into TM bowl and mill **20 sec/speed 10**.

4. When dough has risen, roll out into large rectangle. Allow to rise again for 10 minutes, covered with a clean cloth.

5. Dot the surface of the dough with softened butter and then spread the sugar mixture across evenly. Roll up, into a long sausage shape and cut through in 5cm thick rounds. Place cut side up in greased baking dish. Allow to rise again for 30 minutes.

6. Meanwhile, preheat oven to 200°C.

7. When scrolls have risen sufficiently so that they touch each other, place into oven and bake for 20–25 minutes until golden and fragrant. While they are baking, make frosting.

8. Place all ingredients into TM bowl and blend **10 sec/speed 5**. Scrape down sides of bowl and repeat.

9. Spread over scrolls while they are still warm, not hot! Eat the same day…(as if I have to tell you that!)

To dry a vanilla bean, place into 140°C oven for around 1 hour. Do several at a time if possible. This will make the vanilla bean brittle and it will mill very easily into a fragrant powder.

QUINOA AND SPELT CRACKERS

Call me crackers, but there is nothing more rewarding than making your own crackers. Crunchy, seeded, salty … cue the cheese, or dip, or pesto and Bob's your uncle. You are feeling like a real pro foodie. Thanks, Uncle Bob… whoever you are.

NEED

- 1 sprig rosemary, foliage only
- 100g quinoa
- 100g spelt flour
- 100g plain flour
- 100g water
- 50g EVOO
- 2 tbsp seeds of choice
- Good pinch coarse sea salt

DO

1. Preheat oven to 180°C. Line 2–3 trays with baking paper.

2. Place rosemary, quinoa, spelt and plain flours, water and EVOO into TM bowl and blend **6 sec/speed 6**.

3. Add seeds and salt and knead **1 min/Interval**.

4. Divide dough into 4 parts. Roll each portion out between 2 sheets of baking paper to as thin as possible. Transfer to baking tray and score surface with pizza wheel. Bake for 20 minutes.

5. Break apart when cool.

6. Repeat with each portion of dough.

7. Return all cooked crackers to the turned off oven for as long as it takes to get them to be 'crackers'! They should snap and be crunchy.

LEMON PARMESAN WAFERS

16–20 WAFERS

The little wafer that could! You will just love these for the quickest little dress-the-cheese-platter-upper-er ever! Whip up a batch in no time! SO impressive.

NEED

- Zest 1 lemon
- 100g parmesan
- 2 tsp corn flour

DO

1. Preheat oven to 170°C and line a baking tray with paper.

2. Place all ingredients into TM and mill **10 sec/speed 8**. Place spoonfuls onto tray and bake for 6-7 minutes or until golden and crispy around the edges.

3. Place warm wafers over a rolling pin or other cylindrical object until cold to achieve the curved shape.

TASTE

- Serve as part of a cheese platter, with pesto, dips or as an accompaniment to soup.

PIZZA DOUGH

MAKES 2 THICK CRUSTS OR 4 THIN CRUSTS

NEED

- 30g fresh yeast
- 2 tsp Powdered Malt (see page 26)
- 300g water
- 30g EVOO
- 500g bakers flour
- Pinch sea salt

DO

1. Place yeast, malt, water and EVOO into TM bowl and warm **2 min/37°C/speed 2**.

2. Add remaining ingredients and blend **6 sec/speed 6**. Knead **3 min/Interval**.

3. Turn out onto floured Silpat mat and form into a tight ball. Wrap and allow to rise for 10–15 minutes for thin crust. If you are aiming for a thick crust, allow it to rise for at least 30 minutes before using.

SCENTED VANILLA BEAN PASTRY

NEED

- 50g sugar
- ½ vanilla bean
- 200g cold unsalted butter, cubed
- 380g plain flour
- Ice cold water as needed

DO

1. Place sugar and vanilla bean into TM bowl and mill **10 sec/speed 10**.

2. Add butter and flour and mix **10 sec/speed 6** until resembles breadcrumbs.

3. Add water through hole in lid while you continue to mix **10 sec/Interval** speed. As soon as the dough starts to form a ball, stop and remove pastry from bowl onto lightly floured Silpat mat.

4. Roll and use as directed.

FLAKY BUTTER PASTRY

NEED

- 120g + 120g cold unsalted butter, cubed
- 280g bakers flour
- Pinch sea salt
- 3 tsp lemon juice
- 15–20g icy water

DO

1. Place 120g butter into TM bowl and chop **4 sec/speed 5**. Place into freezer on a plate or shallow bowl.

2. Place remaining pastry ingredients except water into TM bowl and blend **5 sec/speed 6**. You should have a breadcrumb look.

3. Add enough water to just bring mixture together. This will depend on the weather and the flour you use.

4. Blend **10 sec/speed 7**. Remove dough and roll out into a rectangle (approx. 15x30cm) on floured Silpat mat.

5. Fold each end of the pastry over on top of itself in thirds. Turn the pastry so that the folded edges are on each side of your Silpat mat.

6. Roll again and repeat this process 3–4 times. If the dough becomes sticky at any point, stop, wrap and place into the fridge until easy to work with again. The dough should eventually be in a beautiful even brick shape. Wrap and refrigerate for at least 30 minutes.

7. Remove butter from freezer and pastry from fridge. Roll pastry out again as above, but between each folded layer, sprinkle the frozen chopped butter. You should divide the butter into approx. 4 to do this process, so you get 2 turns of the pastry block, with butter in between each layer. (This is called laminating and is your key to awesome pastry…the more layers with butter in between, the better your 'flake' will be!)

8. Return pastry to the fridge for at least another 30 minutes before removing, rolling and proceeding with the recipe of choice.

9. You can use this pastry for so many recipes in this book, but don't stop there. Wrap sausages, stuffed chicken breast rolls, marzipan, chocolate and cheesecake mixtures in pastry, brush with egg wash, bake and you have died and gone to heaven.

SOUPER BOWL

The best thing about winter is the soups…there is nothing more homely or inviting on a rainy Sunday (or any other day) than a fresh loaf of homemade bread and some health-giving chunky or smooth, quick, fragrant, tasty, steaming, one-bowl wonderful soup straight from your TM. It's (almost) enough to make you wish it was winter all year round!

CHORIZO, FRENCH LENTIL AND SWEET POTATO SOUP

SERVES 4–6

This hearty soup has all the charm of good, healthy farmhouse food, best served before a blazing open fire, with crusty bread, some rough red wine and in ceramic bowls. Ahhh, soup as it was meant to be.

NEED

- 50g French green lentils
- 260g water
- 200g brown onion, cut in pieces
- 2 cloves garlic
- 260g chorizo sausage, sliced
- 700g sweet potato, diced 2–3cm
- 90g Umami Paste (see page 9)
- 750g liquid stock

Garnish
- 30g lemon juice, fresh
- Zest 1 lemon, finely grated
- Italian parsley to taste

DO

1. Place lentils and water into TM bowl and cook **30 min/100°C/speed 1**. Remove from bowl and set aside.

2. Place onion and garlic into TM bowl and chop **3 sec/speed 5**. Scrape down sides of bowl and add chorizo. Sauté **5 min/Varoma/Reverse + speed 1**.

3. Add remaining ingredients, including cooked lentils and cook **15 min/100°C/Reverse + speed 1**.

4. Serve with lemon juice, lemon zest and snipped parsley to taste.

PRAWN AND CORN GUMBO

SERVES 4–6

I tossed up calling this a stew but when I did I was severely told off on Twitter by the foodies I call friends, who insisted that it is a gumbo. So gumbo it is. A gumbo is a hearty, spicy soup or stew from the deep south of the US, with a roux as its beginning. Regardless of its origin, this recipe is fragrant and delicious. If you are not a big seafood fan, try cubed ham or bacon in place of the prawns.

NEED

- 100g unsalted butter, cubed
- 20g flour
- 3 cloves garlic
- 250g brown onions, cut in pieces
- 170g celery, sliced
- 4–6 spring onions/shallots, sliced
- 100g green capsicum, diced (approx. 1 medium)

- 2 bay leaves
- 1 tsp sea salt
- 35g dry sherry
- 170g water
- 1 tbsp veggie stock paste
- 1 pinch dried chilli flakes
- 1 tsp ground paprika
- 600g raw prawns, peeled and deveined

- 120g corn kernels, fresh
- 50g lemon juice, fresh
- Few sprigs flat leaf parsley, snipped

DO

1. Place butter and flour into TM bowl and cook **5 min/Varoma/speed 3**.

2. Add garlic and onions and chop **4 sec/speed 7**.

3. Add celery, spring onions, capsicum, bay leaves and salt and cook **5 min/100°C/Reverse + speed 1**.

4. Add sherry, water, stock paste, chilli flakes, paprika and prawns and cook **5 min/100°C/Reverse + speed 1**.

5. Add corn and lemon juice and a little of the parsley, reserving some for garnish.

6. Cook **3 min/100°C/Reverse + speed 1**. Serve on its own or with steamed rice and additional parsley.

This is a pumpkin soup recipe with a difference, moving it up a notch to ambrosial comfort food. Knock up a batch of rolls to go with it and you are guaranteed some oohs and ahhs. Good on you, mum..

CURRIED BUTTERNUT SOUP

SERVES 4–6

NEED

- 50g Yellow Curry Paste
  (see page 7)
- 1 tbsp tamarind paste
- 2 onions, quartered
- 1 tbsp EVOO
- 2 tbsp Umami Paste (see page 9)
- 500g butternut pumpkin,
  cut in pieces
- 400ml can coconut milk
- 500g water or stock of choice
- 2 pinches sea salt or to taste

Garnish
- Coconut slices
- Chopped coriander

DO

1. Place Yellow Curry Paste, tamarind paste, onions and oil into TM bowl and blend **2 sec/speed 6**. Scrape down sides of bowl.

2. Sauté **2 min/Varoma/speed 2**.

3. Add remaining ingredients except garnishes and cook **15 min/100°C/speed 2**.

4. Allow to rest in TM bowl 1–2 minutes. Blend **30 sec/speed 8**, bringing speed up slowly to avoid spatter.

5. Serve hot in large bowls with shaved coconut slices and chopped coriander.

TOMATO AND LEEK SOUP

SERVES 4–6

Tomato soup is a staple in my household and it has been a loooong time since it came out of a can. It is fast to make and always tastes amazing. Add some fresh bread and you have a wonderful lunch in no time or a light dinner for a quiet night in. And even better, you know exactly what you're eating….no nasty numbers here!

NEED

- 1 leek, cleaned and chopped (200–250g)
- 20g EVOO
- 600g tomatoes, chopped
- 40g Umami Paste (see page 9)
- 40g veggie stock concentrate
- 50g tomato paste (1 sachet)
- 1 tsp Citrus Olive Salt (see page 11)

- Zest 1 orange, finely grated
- 85g fresh orange juice
- 400g water
- Handful basil leaves
- Handful parsley leaves

DO

1. Place leek and EVOO into TM bowl and chop **3 sec/speed 5**.

2. Sauté **5 min/Varoma/speed 2**.

3. Add remaining ingredients and cook **14 min/100°C /speed 2**.

4. Blend **1 min/speed 5–6**, bringing speed up slowly to avoid spatter.

5. Serve hot with a dollop of crème fraiche or mascarpone cheese and freshly cracked black pepper.

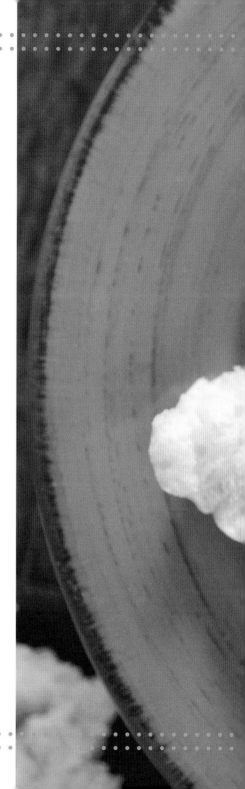

SAGE, POTATO AND LEEK SOUP

SERVES 4–6

I have a fantastic herb garden that is full of sage every spring. I dry it, I fry it, trim it, gift it and I love to use it in almost everything savoury. I have yet to try sage ice-cream, but never say never! This soup was born one cold spring day when soup was just the antidote to rain and bluster. The sage had already sprung to life from its woody wintery self and I just couldn't resist adding it to a steaming pot of yumminess! If you don't have fresh sage, use dried – and plant some now!

NEED

- Handful fresh sage leaves
- 1 leek, cleaned and sliced
- 30g unsalted butter, cubed
- 4 potatoes, cubed (500–550g)
- 600g water
- 2 tbsp Chicken Stock Powder (see page 25)
- White pepper and sea salt to taste

DO

1. Place sage, leek and butter into TM bowl and cook **7 min/Varoma/speed 1**.

2. Add remaining ingredients and cook **15 min/100°C/speed 1**.

3. Check the potatoes are cooked before blending **1 min/speed 9**. If potatoes are not quite crumbling with the pressure from the back of a fork, cook a further **3 min/100°C/speed 1**, then proceed with blending.

4. Adjust seasoning to taste and serve with fresh sage sprigs and of course a drizzle of cream if desired.

A BIT ON THE SIDE

It's often the side dishes that take centre stage and that's true of this little collection. Yummy in their own right, they provide the crowning touch to a great meal or can be perfect for a light lunch. Add a salad and crusty bread to most of them, invite the girls around and I am confident there will be no complaints…

BRAISED BRUSSELS SPROUTS WITH SPECK AND VERJUICE REDUCTION

SERVES 4–6

No more complaining about eating your brussels sprouts…seriously. You must eat this dish immediately, though, as the sprouts do become a little bitter. If you could ever call brussels sprouts decadent, cooking them like this would be one way. Totally fantastic. One of my better vegetable moments.

NEED

- 60g pine nuts, toasted
- 200g verjuice
- Cracked black pepper
- 60g unsalted butter, cubed
- 170g speck, cubed
- 600g brussels sprouts, peeled and halved
- Sea salt to taste

DO

1. Place verjuice and pepper into small saucepan and cook on a medium to low heat (Induction 6) until reduced and syrupy.

2. Add butter and stir through until melted. Set aside.

3. Place speck into TM bowl and cook **8 min/Varoma/Reverse + speed 1**.

4. Add brussels sprouts and cook **12 min/100°C/Reverse + speed 1**.

5. Pour verjuice reduction over and stir through **4 sec/Reverse + speed 1**.

6. Keep hot until ready to serve, sprinkled with toasted pine nuts.

ARTICHOKE AND POTATO GRATINS

SERVES 6–8

NEED

- 160g brown onions, cut in pieces
- 2 large cloves garlic
- 50g Swiss cheese, cubed
- 50g parmesan cheese, cubed
- 50g mild cheese, cubed

- 500g potatoes
- 6–8 marinated artichoke hearts, drained & halved
- 300ml cream

- Citrus Olive Salt to taste (see page 11)

DO

① Preheat oven to fan-forced 160°C. Butter 6–8 ramekin dishes and set aside on a baking tray.

② Place onions into TM bowl and chop **3 sec/speed 5**. Remove from bowl and set aside in a large bowl.

③ Finely slice the potatoes and toss them through the onions.

④ Place garlic and all cheeses into TM bowl and mill **8 sec/speed 8**.

⑤ Divide half of the potato and onion mixture between ramekins, making sure the potato sits flat in each dish.

⑥ Divide half the cheese mixture and half the cream between ramekins.

⑦ Place two artichoke hearts in each dish.

⑧ Top with remaining potato and cream. Finish with cheese and a sprinkle of salt.

⑨ Cover each ramekin with aluminum foil, shiny side down and bake for 60 minutes.

⑩ Cook in 10 minute increments until you are happy that the potatoes are well cooked. (Test with a skewer.)

⑪ Increase heat of oven to 180°C, remove foil and bake for a further 20 minutes until golden. Serve immediately with a little sprinkling of Gremolata as a side dish to roasted meat and fish.

GREMOLATA

NEED

- 2 cloves garlic
- Zest 1 lemon
- 30g parmesan
- 30g pine nuts, toasted
- Few Italian parsley leaves

DO

1. Place garlic, zest and parmesan into TM bowl and mill **10 sec/speed 8**. Add pine nuts and parsley and blend **3 sec/speed 7**.

2. Use as garnish for anything you like. Especially good on tomato-based meat dishes, such as lasagne, bolognaise, Osso Bucco or even try it on Pork and Spicy Sausage Ragu in place of plain parmesan.

CHEESY SAGED POLENTA

SERVES 6

This is a fantastic option to accompany most main meals instead of rice, potatoes or pasta. I just love polenta and cooked in the TM is absolutely the easiest way. No more standing over a spitting pot, stirring it within an inch of its life to prevent those lumps and bumps that are part of the bad rap that polenta has earned over the years. Add as much flavour as you like in the shape of herbs and cheeses, or aromatics like onions and garlic. And don't forget the butter – lots of it. Try this once and you will officially become a polenta fan.

NEED

- 100g parmesan, cubed
- 100g mozzarella, cubed
- Handful sage leaves, stalks removed
- 2 tsp sea salt

- 60g Umami Paste (see page 9)
- 200g polenta
- 400g liquid stock of choice
- 60g unsalted butter, cubed

DO

1. Place cheeses and sage leaves into TM bowl and mill **10 sec/speed 10**. Remove from bowl and set aside.

2. Place salt, Umami Paste, polenta and stock into TM bowl and cook **8 min/100°C/speed 4**.

3. Add cheese mixture and butter and blend **1 min/speed 4**.

4. Serve immediately, garnished with additional sage leaves.

BROAD BEAN AND PEA SALAD WITH BOCCONCINI

SERVES 8

Salads are really a big part of how we eat in Australia and this is another method to file away. Use heaps of iced water in the biggest bowl you can muster in which to plunge the cooked vegies. This stops the cooking and preserves the beauty of the bright colours of the vegetables. Bring on the best EVOO possible and a little flavoured salt of choice from your TM pantry – a great way to dine in style on any vegetables.

NEED

- 1L water
- 200g peas, fresh or frozen
- 400g broad beans, fresh or frozen
- 2L iced water in large bowl
- Handful each basil, mint, flat-leaf parsley

- 1 lemon, finely grated zest and juice
- 30g EVOO, plus extra for drizzling
- ½ bunch chives, chopped
- Salt and pepper to taste

- 8 baby mozzarella (bocconcini), coarsely torn

DO

1. Place water into TM bowl and bring to the boil **8 min/Varoma/speed 3**.

2. Place vegetables into steamer dish and tray. Set steamer into position and steam **7 min/Varoma/speed 3**.

3. Remove vegetables and plunge into iced water immediately. Skin broad beans if desired.

4. Dry TM bowl and place herbs into TM bowl and chop **3 sec/speed 6**.

5. Add EVOO, lemon juice and seasoning and blend **3 sec/speed 4**.

6. Toss together with remaining ingredients, drizzle with extra EVOO and serve with crusty bread.

The ingredients I use in my recipes are readily available, so please do not scour the southern-most slopes of the Andes to find red rice. Feel free to use any rice you choose. The delightful thing about red rice, however, is that it is a little chewy. It never collapses into a gluggy lump of starch and you will enjoy its unique properties in this recipe.

MINTED RED RICE AND CHICK PEA SALAD

SERVES 6–8

NEED

- 150g red rice
- 1L water
- 1 tbsp peppercorns
- Handful mint leaves
- Handful Italian parsley
- 3 cloves garlic
- 2 spring onions/shallots, sliced
- 40g soy sauce or tamari
- 40g lemon juice, fresh
- 20g rice wine vinegar
- 2 tsp raw sugar
- Pinch sea salt
- 100g EVOO

- 1 red capsicum, diced
- 2 stalks celery, sliced
- 200g Lebanese cucumber, diced
- 400g tin chick peas, drained
- 100g pistachios
- 50g pumpkin seeds
- 50g craisins (dried cranberries)

DO

1. Place rice into simmering basket and insert into TM bowl.

2. Pour water over the rice and cook **30 min/100°C/speed 3**.

3. Remove rice, cool. Drain water from bowl.

4. Place peppercorns into clean, dry TM bowl and mill **5 sec/speed 9**.

5. Add mint, parsley, garlic, spring onions/shallots, soy sauce, lemon juice, sugar, salt and EVOO and blend **10 sec/speed 8**.

6. Place remaining ingredients into a large salad bowl and toss dressing through. Add rice and toss again just to coat with dressing.

7. Serve garnished with additional mint leaves.

STEAMED SPINACH WITH HAZELNUT AND FENNEL DRESSING

SERVES 4

This is a shipload of spinach (you heard me), but it wilts down to enough for 4 decent servings. It's easy to up the ante for more servings by increasing the dressing by a third and adding 100g spinach per serving. You will enjoy this as a special occasion side dish, but if you struggle to get your daily five serves, it is a great way eat a whole… well, a shipload of good-for-you greens. The dressing can be served on any salad and will keep in the fridge for around 3 weeks. The nuts should only be added just before serving for crunch factor.

NEED

- 1 tsp fennel seeds
- 2 cloves garlic
- 1 tsp Dijon mustard
- Juice 1 orange
- 70g EVOO

- 70g hazelnuts, roasted and skinned
- 400g baby spinach leaves
- 1L boiling water

DO

1. Place fennel seeds into TM bowl and dry roast **10 min/Varoma/speed 1**.

2. Add garlic, mustard, orange juice and EVOO and blend **10 sec/speed 6**.

3. Add hazelnuts and blend **3 sec/speed 5**. Remove from bowl and set aside.

4. Place ½ the spinach into steamer dish. Pour water into TM bowl and set steamer into position. Cook **5 min/Varoma/speed 4**. Add remaining spinach and cook **5 min/Varoma/speed 4**.

5. Toss dressing through and serve warm. Garnish with a few additional chopped hazelnuts.

TASTE

- Toss the dressing through a salad of fresh baby spinach, sliced fennel and red onion.
- Garnish with a few segments of peeled orange.

KALE AND PARMESAN SALAD

SERVES 6

OK, I've broken my cardinal rule about only using accessible ingredients but for such a tasty result, you will forgive me. Nicolas Poelaert, a Melbourne chef with amazing talents which he displays in his Embrasse kitchen, shared this dressing recipe with me and although it is tweaked a little, I just loved the addition of the pine needles. But if you don't feel like foraging in the forest, this recipe is just as delicious without them.

NEED

Dressing
- Fresh pine needle tips (only available in spring time)
- 1 sprig rosemary, leaves only
- Pinch sea salt
- 40g white wine vinegar
- 20g honey

- 80g EVOO
- Juice 1 lemon
- 75g parmesan, cubed

Salad
- 1 bunch Kale, veins removed
- 60g red onion, cut in pieces

- 50g pine nuts, toasted
- Extra shaved parmesan for garnish

DO

1. Place pine tips, rosemary and salt into TM bowl and mill **5 sec/speed 7**.

2. Add vinegar and honey and heat **2 min/90°C/speed 1**.

3. Add remaining dressing ingredients and blend **5 sec/speed 8**.

4. Without removing the dressing, place half the kale into the bowl. With the aid of the spatula, chop **5 sec/speed 4**. Remove kale with a pair of tongs (leaving as much dressing in the bottom of the bowl as possible) and place in a large bowl.

5. Place onion and the other half of the kale into TM bowl and chop **5 sec/speed 4**. Add to bowl and toss gently to combine. Place onto platter, garnish with toasted pine nuts and shaved parmesan. Serve immediately.

JACKET POTATOES AND PESTO SOUR CREAM

I bet you didn't know you could do jacket potatoes in the TM, did you? Technically they are finished in the dry heat of an oven, which gives the nice skin that we are accustomed to, but pre-steaming means they retain their shape (great for presentation), flavour (great for your diners) and nutrients (great for your body). You could even pre-steam them a few days in advance, before finishing them off in the oven just before serving – a great timesaver. As for Pesto Sour Cream – I could package and market it, but it would never taste as good as this. Aren't you glad you have a TM?

NEED

- 1 red skinned potato per person
- 1L water
- Handful fresh Italian parsley
- 50g pesto of choice

- 30g Umami Paste (see page 9)
- 200g sour cream or crème fraiche
- Juice 1 lemon

DO

1. Preheat oven to 200°C.

2. Prick each potato with a skewer and wrap in foil. Place in steamer dish and tray. Pour water into TM bowl and set steamer into position. Steam **25 min/Varoma/speed 4**. Test that potatoes are cooked. (This may vary depending on the size and variety of potato used.)

3. When done, transfer potatoes to oven tray and place into oven while you make the topping.

4. Place parsley into clean dry TM bowl and chop **3 sec/speed 7**.

5. Add remaining ingredients and blend **3 sec/speed 6**. Chill until ready to serve.

6. Remove potatoes from oven when ready to serve and top with Pesto Sour Cream.

TASTE

- Pesto Sour Cream makes an excellent salad dressing or dip with crudités.

THE MAIN EVENT

This chapter is full of fantastic ideas and suggestions to feed your family and friends, from light meals to a full-on main meal for a hungry mob. I love salads, so yes, there are plenty of those. I also love Mexican and Asian cuisine so there is a good dash of those flavours as well. Mostly simple, quick and all delicious, they come from our family table to yours. I hope you enjoy them.

BEEF AND ALE PIE

SERVES 6–8

There are no surprises here – just good, old-fashioned, yummy comfort food.
It may not be pretty (though our lovely picture suggests otherwise), but who
cares, serve it up and let's eat!

NEED

- 5 cloves garlic
- 320g brown onions, cut in pieces
- 20g EVOO
- 350g portobello or brown mushrooms, sliced
- 1 sprig rosemary, stalks removed
- 120g pale ale
- 800g–1kg gravy beef, cubed
- 2 tbsp corn flour
- Freshly ground black pepper to taste

- 30g fish sauce
- 60g Umami Paste (see page 9)
- 1 bay leaf
- 1 batch Flaky Butter Pastry (see page 54) OR 2–3 sheets commercial puff pastry
- Egg wash

DO

1. Place garlic, onions and EVOO into TM bowl and chop **2 sec/speed 4**. Scrape down sides of bowl and sauté **5 min/Varoma/speed 1**.

2. Add remaining ingredients except pastry and egg wash and cook **60 min/90°C/Reverse + speed 1**. Cool slightly.

3. Preheat oven to 200°C.

4. Pour pie filling into deep-sided ceramic pie or baking dish.

5. Cover with pastry and seal edges. Brush with egg wash and bake for 30–40 minutes until golden and puffed.

6. Serve with steamed vegetables and jacket potatoes.

In all the years of loving fresh Mexican food, I can never go past the simplicity, or speed, of a Taco Salad. Make your own tortilla wedges, or just buy your favourite corn chips to serve. With a few pantry items on hand, you can have this on the table in no time. Try it with pork, chicken or even fish...though shredding the fish will hardly be necessary, and shorten the cooking time accordingly.

SHREDDED BEEF TACO SALAD

SERVES 6–8

NEED

Dressing
- Handful coriander leaves
- 1 red chilli
- 1 clove garlic
- 1 tsp raw sugar
- ½ tsp ground cumin
- 1 tsp Chilli Lime Salt (see page 11)
- Black pepper to taste
- 60g lime juice, fresh
- 100g EVOO

Beef
- 500g beef steak, cut into large pieces
- 1L beef stock
- Sea salt and pepper to taste

Salad
- 150g cheese, cubed
- Iceberg lettuce, torn into pieces as needed
- 400g tin kidney beans, drained and rinsed

- 100g black olives, sliced
- Few spring onions/shallots, sliced
- 250g punnet grape tomatoes, halved
- 1 red capsicum, diced
- 1–2 avocados, pitted and diced
- Toasted tortilla wedges
- Sour cream to serve (optional)

DO

1. To make dressing place coriander, chilli and garlic into TM bowl and chop **5 sec/speed 6**.

2. Add remaining dressing ingredients and blend **10 sec/speed 6**. Remove from bowl and set aside.

3. Without washing bowl, place beef into simmering basket and insert into TM bowl. Pour stock over and cook **20 min/100°C/speed 2**. Drain stock and reserve for another use.

4. Place cooked beef into TM bowl and shred **5 sec/Reverse/speed 6**.

5. To assemble salad, place cheese into clean and dry TM bowl and grate **8 sec/speed 9**. Remove from bowl and set aside.

6. Arrange lettuce over the bottom of a shallow serving dish or platter.

7. Spoon beef mixture evenly over lettuce and then top with layers of beans, olives, spring onions, tomatoes, capsicum and avocados. Finish with tortilla wedges and drizzle with dressing just before serving.

8. Dollop with sour cream (if desired).

CRIO BRÜ BEEF CHILLI

SERVES 6–8

'Chocolate in Chilli', I hear you cry… let's discuss it. Mexican cuisine has used chocolate in savoury dishes for centuries because, of course, chocolate is not sweet in nature. It is only after the addition of sugar and milk fat that chocolate goes from being a fantastic superfood to a western version only distantly related to the original, and with no health-giving properties. So give this recipe a try. Crio Brü gives a depth of flavour that will make you come back for more. In fact, the first time I made this my daughter asked me wistfully if I would teach her to cook. I told her she could take a TM and my cookbook with her when she left home and all would be well.

NEED

- 2 red chillies
- 200g red onion, cut in pieces
- 6–8 cloves garlic
- 250g bacon, cut in pieces
- 1 tsp each ground cinnamon, allspice, coriander, cumin, paprika
- Coarse sea salt to taste
- Freshly ground black pepper to taste
- 1kg beef, 4cm cubed
- 170g brewed Crio Brü liquid
- 2 tbsp Crio Brü granules
- 100g beer or ale
- 2 tbsp balsamic vinegar
- Steamed rice to serve
- Sour cream to serve (optional)

DO

① Chargrill chillies over an open flame and place into a glass bowl. Cover with plastic wrap and allow to sweat. Rub skins off when flesh is cool.

② Place chillies, onion, garlic, bacon, spices, salt and pepper into TM bowl and chop **4 sec/speed 5**.

③ Sauté **5 min/Varoma/speed 1**.

④ Add remaining ingredients and cook **60 min/90°C/Reverse + speed 1** with MC off. Use simmering basket on top of lid to prevent spatter.

⑤ Serve over steamed rice with Tomato and Avocado Salsa and a dollop of sour cream if desired.

TOMATO AND AVOCADO SALSA

NEED

- 1 punnet grape tomatoes
- 1 avocado
- 1–2 spring onions/ shallots
- Few sprigs coriander
- 1 tsp Citrus Olive Salt (see page 11)
- Lemon juice to taste

DO

1. Slice tomatoes, dice avocado and slice onions. Toss with remaining ingredients. Serve as a garnish with the Crio Brü Beef Chilli.

I am a big fan of charring and roasting to add essential flavour, something clearly not possible in the TM. I usually roast nuts prior to use in a recipe and, as in this recipe, a charred capsicum or chilli or tortilla. The flavour is completely different from the fresh or uncharred version. But if you prefer to use the uncharred versions, do so.

CHARRED PEPPER AND CHORIZO FAJITAS

SERVES 6–10

My version of Mexican food is light on the cheese and sour cream and more about the fresh herbs and flavours. I do have a large family and I love this recipe because I can feed a crowd with little effort, simply by adding extra rice, sweet potato or salad items. I lay it all out, and they help themselves (again and again, and sometimes, again).

NEED

- 150g long grain rice
- 300g sweet potato, peeled and cubed (approx. 1–2cm square)
- 1 tsp Chilli Lime Salt (see page 11)
- 1L water
- 1 red chilli

- 1 red capsicum
- 150g mild cheese of choice, (gouda, edam, cheddar)
- 5 cloves garlic
- 150g red onion, cut in pieces
- 300g chorizo sausage, sliced
- Juice 1 lime

- 7–8 flour tortillas
- Salad greens of choice
- Chopped coriander
- Kalamata olives to garnish

DO

1. Place rice into simmering basket and insert into TM bowl. Place sweet potato into steamer dish. Sprinkle with Chilli Lime Salt. Pour water over rice, place steamer into position.

2. Cook **15 min/Varoma/speed 3**. Set aside and empty water from bowl.

3. While the rice and potato are cooking, char the chilli and red capsicum over a low naked flame until totally black. This will take approx. 15 minutes for the capsicum. Place into a glass bowl, cover with plastic wrap and cool. Rub skin off and de-seed chilli if desired. If you would rather avoid this process, use them both fresh or see across.

4. Place cheese into TM bowl and chop **5 sec/speed 8**. Remove from bowl and set aside.

5. Place chilli, garlic and onion into TM bowl and chop **2 sec/speed 6**. Scrape down sides of bowl. Add chorizo and lime juice and sauté **10 min/Varoma/Reverse + speed 1**.

6. Heat one tortilla at a time over a direct flame for 10–15 seconds on each side, or in a dry hot frypan.

7. Divide the chorizo mix between tortillas, add a little rice, sweet potato, top with grated cheese and fresh greens. Cut roasted capsicum into strips and arrange on top, then snip some coriander over the whole thing. Wrap tightly and eat immediately.

CHORIZO AND POTATO SAVOURY FRITTATA

SERVES 6

This is a great recipe to make ahead for a lazy Sunday brunch with friends, and will keep for up to 3–4 days in the fridge. It is delicious hot or cold, and the tomato sauce is fantastic by itself. Simply reheat the frittata…and you are going to want more of that sauce. Now, where did I put those dried chillies?

NEED

Sauce
- 2 dried red chillies
- 4 cloves garlic
- 1 tsp cumin seeds
- 20g EVOO
- 500g tomatoes, quartered
- 1 tsp Chilli Lime Salt (see page 11)
- 1 tbsp dark brown sugar

Frittata
- 600g red skinned potatoes
- 100g red onion, cut in pieces
- 300g chorizo, cut in pieces
- 1 punnet grape tomatoes
- 6 eggs
- 300g cream

- 1 tsp Chilli Lime Salt (see page 11)
- 1 tsp freshly cracked black pepper

DO

1. Place chillies, garlic, cumin and EVOO into TM bowl and chop **5 sec/speed 4**. Scrape down sides of bowl and sauté **6 min/Varoma/speed 1**. Add tomatoes, Chilli Lime Salt and sugar to bowl.

2. Prepare potatoes by slicing into 1cm thick slices (without peeling) and placing into steamer dish. Set steamer into position and steam over sauce as you cook **20 min/Varoma/speed 3**.

3. Place potatoes into an oiled ovenproof dish and set aside. Scrape out sauce and set aside. Rinse bowl.

4. Preheat oven to fan-forced 160°C.

5. Place red onions, and chorizo into TM bowl and chop **8 sec/speed 8**. Scrape down sides of bowl and cook **7 min/Varoma/speed 1**.

6. Spoon across potatoes. Top with tomato sauce and spread evenly.

7. Slice grape tomatoes in half and arrange across the top of the sauce.

8. Place eggs, cream and seasoning into TM bowl and blend **10 sec/speed 10**.

9. Pour over chorizo and tomatoes. Bake for 50–60 minutes or until puffed and golden, and set in the centre.

Serve hot or cold, with salad or as a breakfast slice. Add asparagus spears instead of grape tomatoes. To make it less spicy, use fewer chillies in your tomato sauce, or use a milder cured sausage in place of chorizo.

PORK AND SAUSAGE RAGU

SERVES 6–8

When my kids were young, we ate pasta….a LOT. It was filling for growing boys and easy to cook. The variety of ways you can use pasta is endless, and this recipe is a family favourite. Different sausages will give you a different flavour every time, and if you make your own passata, you have limitless options just waiting in the fridge. Open it and see what's there …

NEED

- 250g spicy cured sausage of choice, cut in pieces
- 5 cloves garlic
- 250g brown onions, cut in pieces
- 800–1kg pork fillet, diced, 6–8cm
- 400g tomato passata
- 100g dry red wine
- 40g Umami Paste (see page 9)

- Good pinch sea salt
- Freshly cracked black pepper
- 3 bay leaves
- Pasta and grated parmesan to serve

DO

1. Place sausage and garlic into TM bowl and chop **5 sec/speed 8**. Add onions and chop **2 sec/speed 6**.

2. Sauté **5 min/Varoma/speed 1**.

3. Add remaining ingredients and cook **30 min/90°C/Reverse + speed 2**.

4. Serve with cooked short pasta and lots of grated parmesan or pecorino cheese.

LAMB PESTO CRUSTO WITH GUSTO

SERVES 6–8

NEED

- Lamb roasting piece of choice
- Few coloured peppercorns to taste
- Zest 1 lemon
- 5 cloves garlic
- Handful mint and basil leaves
- Few sprigs rosemary, foliage only
- Handful rocket or Mizuna leaves

- 100g pistachio kernels
- Citrus Olive Salt to taste (see page 11)
- 30g lemon juice, fresh
- Enough EVOO to bring it all together

DO

1. Place lamb into oven bag and cook in pre-heated HOT oven for 20–30 minutes (depending on size of roast).

2. Meanwhile place peppercorns, garlic and herbs into TM bowl and mill **8 sec/speed 8**.

3. Add remaining ingredients except oil and blend **5 sec/speed 8**. Scrape down with spatula if necessary.

4. With blades rotating on **speed 3**, add enough oil through lid to just bring the mix to a solid paste.

5. When lamb is nearly cooked to taste, remove from oven bag, coat with pesto and return to oven for a further 10–15 minutes, until crust is fragrant and golden.

6. Serve with sides of choice.

CURRIED CHICKEN SANDWICH FILLING

SERVES 6

This recipe is another carry-over from my American days. Grapes are best, but the tartness of cherries is also fantastic. Of course the Curry Mayo is a story all by itself, but if you cannot be bothered making it, just use ordinary mayonnaise with a little curry powder mixed through.

NEED

- 2 chicken breast fillets, cut into large pieces
- 800g water
- 200g Curry Mayonnaise (see page 20)
- 300g red seedless grapes OR 100g dried cherries

- Few sprigs fresh tarragon or Italian parsley
- 2 stalks celery, sliced on an angle
- 80g walnut pieces, toasted
- 2 spring onions/shallots, sliced

- A few baby spinach leaves
- Pita bread

DO

1. Place chicken into simmering basket and insert into TM bowl. Add water to bowl and cook **13 min/100°C/ speed 3**. Check that chicken is cooked. Add a couple of minutes if necessary though the chicken should not be dry. Drain bowl, place cooked chicken into bowl with mayonnaise, grapes or cherries and herbs.

2. Blend **4 sec/Reverse + speed 5**. Add celery, walnuts and spring onions and stir through **4 sec/Reverse + speed 3**.

3. Fill Pita bread halves with filling and add a few spinach leaves to taste, or use as sandwich filling with bread of choice.

THAI BASIL CHICKEN WITH CHILLI

SERVES 4–6

Is there ever a Friday night that you just don't want to cook? A night when takeout is the usual solution? You would not be alone, but frankly I just can't face the idea of A) what it costs for takeout, and B) what it tastes like when you get it home. Armed with a chilli, TM and a paper clip (just checking if you are really reading this) I got to it and made a delicious version of something you may find at your local takeaway, but OH. SO. MUCH. Nicer.

NEED

- 1 small birdseye chilli (or more to taste)
- 1 red onion, quartered
- 4 cloves garlic
- 20g palm sugar
- 20g EVOO
- 400ml tin coconut cream
- 30g lime juice, fresh
- 10g fish sauce

- 2 kaffir lime leaves
- 800g chicken breast fillet, cubed
- 1 red capsicum, sliced
- Handful basil leaves
- Steamed rice to serve

DO

① Place chilli, onion, garlic, sugar and EVOO into TM bowl and chop **7 sec/speed 8**. Scrape down and sauté **5 min/Varoma/speed 1**.

② Add coconut cream, lime juice, fish sauce and lime leaves and cook **10 min/100°C/speed 2**.

③ Add chicken and cook **5 min/100°C/Reverse + speed 1**.

④ Add capsicum and basil and cook **2 min/100°C/Reverse + speed 1**.

⑤ Serve hot with steamed rice and a few extra basil leaves and sliced chilli to taste.

CHICKEN RENDANG

SERVES 4–6

This meal can be made with very little effort, and dressed up with a few cinnamon sticks, star anise and herb leaves, it will look amazing and appear as if you are dining in style. The recipe is easily adapted to feed many more. Simply add a chicken piece and more steamed rice per serving to the overall recipe.
There is plenty of sauce to go the distance.

NEED

- 1 tsp cardamom seeds
- 6 kaffir lime leaves
- 2 sticks cinnamon
- 4 whole star anise
- 100g eschalots
- 5 cloves garlic
- 2 stalks lemongrass, white part only

- Thumb-sized piece ginger, peeled
- Thumb-sized piece turmeric, peeled
- 30g palm sugar
- 50g water
- 2 tsp sea salt
- 400ml tin coconut cream

- 4–6 pieces chicken maryland or thigh and breast, skin on

DO

1. Place cardamom, lime leaves, cinnamon and star anise into TM bowl and cook **10 min/Varoma/speed 2**. Remove from bowl and set aside.

2. Place eschalots, garlic, lemongrass, ginger, turmeric, palm sugar and water into TM bowl and blend **1 min/speed 9**.

3. Add spices back into bowl and add salt and coconut cream. Cook **15 min/Varoma/speed 2**.

4. Meanwhile preheat oven to 160°C.

5. Pour a small amount of the sauce into a heavy casserole dish. Arrange chicken in dish and pour remaining sauce over, making sure chicken is well coated.

6. Cover and bake for 90 minutes. Remove cover and increase heat to 200°C. Cook a further 30 minutes until sauce is reduced and a rich caramel colour and chicken skin is crispy.

7. Serve with steamed rice.

STUFFED AND STEAMED
CHICKEN ROLLS

SERVES 6–8

NEED

- 1 chicken breast fillet per serving
- 1 batch pesto of choice (see page 30)
- Handful spinach leaves
- 2–3 bocconcini per breast fillet
- Fresh basil leaves
- 1L water for steaming

Sauce
- 2 tbsp Caramelised Garlic Paste (see page 29)
- 1 punnet grape cherry tomatoes
- Sea salt and black pepper to taste

- 1 tsp raw sugar
- Few basil leaves

DO

1. Butterfly each chicken breast so that you have a wide flat piece of chicken. You can ask your butcher to do this if you are not sure how to do it, but watch him and learn, it is very easy.

2. Place a few spoonfuls of pesto onto the centre piece of each breast and spread. Don't over do it.

3. Place remaining fillings onto chicken and roll each one into a tight roll. Wrap in foil as tightly as possible. The tighter the roll, the better the presentation.

4. Place the rolls into the fridge for an hour or so. You can skip this chilling step if you are in a hurry, but you will get a better presentation if the chicken rolls are chilled.

5. Pour water into TM bowl and place chicken rolls into steamer dish and tray. Set into position and cook **25–30 min/Varoma/speed 3**. Remove a roll and slice through the centre to determine if chicken is cooked. Timing may vary depending on the size of the chicken fillets used, as well as technique in filling and rolling. If the chicken looks a little opaque or uncooked, return to dish and cook **10 min/Varoma/speed 3**.

6. Keep rolls warm whilst you make the sauce.

7. Place all sauce ingredients into clean, dry TM bowl and cook **8 min/70°C/Reverse + speed 1**.

8. Remove foil, and slice rolls into 2–3cm thick slices. Serve with sauce, and a green salad.

TASTE

- Imagine: Prawns, scallops, salmon, ham, bacon, sundried tomatoes, roasted eggplant, blue cheese, camembert, brie, cream cheese, avocado, mushrooms, herbs of choice…the possibilities are endless, so shake it up and stuff a chook fillet!

It was this recipe that helped me begin my journey into food publishing. The very first recipe I ever developed in my Kleenmaid job was a steamed and stuffed chicken breast fillet. They soon became a firm favourite for all my classes and as the story goes, I have never looked back. A slightly different method here, steamed in the TM.

SEAFOOD SALAD WITH CHILLI ORANGE DRESSING

SERVES 6–8

This is perfect for a lazy summer's evening. You can prepare the dressing ahead of time, cook the seafood when ready to eat, then simply toss and serve with a little crusty bread, or some steamed rice. You will wow everybody, and be able to claim that you slaved over a hot TM all day!

NEED

- 400–500g Tasmanian salmon fillet, cubed
- 300g prawns, peeled, tails intact
- 300g white fish fillet of choice, cubed
- 1.5L water
- 100g scallops, roe on
- ½ red onion, thinly sliced
- 3–4 handfuls baby spinach or salad greens of choice
- 1 batch Citrus Dressing
- A few coriander leaves as garnish
- Lemon or lime wedges to serve

CITRUS DRESSING

NEED

- Handful coriander leaves
- 50g EVOO
- 1 green chilli
- 1 red chilli
- 75g fish sauce
- Zest 1 orange, finely grated
- Zest 1 lemon, finely grated
- 50g orange juice, fresh
- 50g lemon juice, fresh
- 4 spring onions/shallots, sliced
- 1 tbsp rice wine vinegar
- Citrus Olive Salt to taste (see page 11)
- Raw sugar to taste

DO

1. Place all seafood except scallops into steamer dish and set aside.

2. Place water into TM bowl and set steamer into position. Cook **8 min/Varoma/speed 3**.

3. Stir scallops gently through cooked seafood and cook **2 min/Varoma/speed 3**. Set aside.

4. Prepare dressing (see across).

5. Arrange red onion and salad leaves on large platter. Top with warm seafood, dressing and garnish with herbs.

DO

1. Place all ingredients into TM bowl and blend **10 sec/speed 6** until just combined. (Don't over mix or you will get an emulsion rather than a dressing.)

2. Use as directed.

This salad is so simple it could almost be called a suggestion. I love fruit in the occasional salad and the pineapple in this adds the piquancy that the salad needs. You can add more spinach, avocado, prawns, peanuts and/or pineapple to suit the numbers but I suggest you go large. It will all be eaten, I promise!

PRAWN, PEANUT AND PINEAPPLE SALAD

SERVES 6

NEED

Dressing
- 3 cloves garlic
- ½ red onion, cut in two
- 50g fish sauce
- Juice 3–4 limes (50–60g)
- 40g EVOO
- 20g palm sugar
- 3 handfuls fresh mint leaves
- Few fresh coriander leaves

- Handful chives, sliced
- 1 large red chilli, thinly sliced

Salad
- 300g peanuts
- 500–600g prawns, peeled, tails intact
- 1L water for steaming
- 1 whole pineapple, peeled, cored and diced

- 1–2 large avocados, peeled and diced
- 250g or more baby spinach leaves

DO

1. Place garlic, onion, fish sauce, lime juice, EVOO, palm sugar, mint and coriander into TM bowl and blend **15 sec/speed 6**.

2. Add chives and chilli and stir through **3 sec/Reverse + speed 3**. Remove from bowl and set aside.

3. Roast peanuts by placing nuts into cold oven set to 200°C and cook for 10 minutes or until fragrant. Cool slightly.

4. Place prawns into steamer tray and dish. Pour water into TM bowl and set steamer into position. Steam **8–10 min/Varoma/speed 4**. Stir prawns and make sure they are cooked through. Add a few minutes cooking time as needed. (Time may vary depending on size of prawns used.)

5. Gently toss salad ingredients together with dressing and add a few extra coriander leaves. Serve immediately.

STEAMED SALMON WITH MANGO PINEAPPLE SALSA

SERVES 4–6

I just love salmon: smoke it, steam it, grill it or sushi it, but hand it over. It is a very good source of omega 3 which we all know we need more of. So regard it as doctor's orders: Eat this twice a week.
You will be feeling better in no time.

NEED

- 1 Tasmanian salmon fillet per person
- Good pinch Citrus Olive Salt (see page 11)
- 1 whole pineapple
- 1 large mango
- 1 red chilli
- 20g palm sugar

- 150g red capsicum, deseeded and quartered
- 150g green capsicum, deseeded and quartered
- 40g red onion
- Handful coriander leaves
- Juice 1 lime, fresh
- 200–400g rice

- 1L water
- Coriander leaves and sliced red chilli to garnish

DO

1. Place salmon fillets onto steamer tray and dish, sprinkle with a little Citrus Olive Salt. Set aside.

2. Dice pineapple and mango and place into large mixing bowl.

3. Place chilli and palm sugar into TM bowl and chop **5 sec/speed 6**. Scrape down sides of bowl.

4. Add capsicums, red onion, coriander and lime juice, as well as another pinch of Citrus Olive Salt.

5. Chop **6 sec/speed 4**, with the aid of the spatula. Turn into bowl with pineapple and mango and toss gently. Taste and adjust seasoning if necessary.

6. Measure rice into simmering basket and insert into TM bowl. Pour water over. Steam rice **10 min/100°C/speed 3**.

7. Set steamer into position and steam salmon **4–5 min/Varoma/speed 4**.

8. Serve salmon on a bed of rice with salsa over. Garnish with coriander leaves and fresh chilli as desired.

9. If you like your salmon well cooked, adjust time to suit. It will not matter if the rice is cooked a little longer.

I did a sneaky on this one and fed it to carnivores without advertising the fact it was vegetarian...and, I am happy to say, not a word was said. No one picked it! I know the object of vegetarianism is not to feel as though you are in fact eating meat, through the benefit of clever substitution, but I have to say, this recipe has now become a firm favourite not because it is vegetarian, but because it tastes fantastic. I hope you enjoy it as well.

QUINOA AND MUSHROOM LASAGNE

SERVES 8–10

NEED

Ragu

- 100g quinoa (I used black & red)
- 40g dried porcini or shitake mushrooms
- 4 tbsp soy or tamari sauce
- 400g boiling water
- Handful basil leaves
- 300–350g brown onions, cut in pieces
- 5 cloves garlic
- 200g red capsicum, cut in pieces
- 30g EVOO

- 200g Swiss brown mushrooms, sliced
- 2 tsp sea salt
- 700g passata or tomato puree
- 10g sugar
- 50g tomato paste (1 sachet)
- 60g Umami Paste (see page 9)

Béchamel

- 80g parmesan cheese, cubed
- 200g cheddar cheese, cubed
- 45g butter

- 40g plain flour
- 2 eggs
- 600g milk
- Pinch freshly grated nutmeg
- Sea salt and freshly cracked black pepper to taste

Assembly

- 250g egg pasta, lasagne sheets

DO

Ragu

1. Place quinoa, dried mushrooms, soy sauce and boiling water into an insulated bowl, cover and allow to soak overnight or for several hours.

2. Remove mushrooms and slice. Return to quinoa and set aside.

3. Place basil into TM bowl and chop **3 sec/speed 6**.

4. Add onions, garlic and EVOO into TM bowl and chop **5 sec/speed 5**.

5. Scrape down sides of bowl and sauté **5 min/Varoma/speed 1**.

6. Add remaining ragu ingredients including quinoa/mushroom mixture with liquid and cook **30 min/90°C/Reverse + speed 2**. Set aside.

7. Preheat oven to 160°C.

Béchamel

1. Place cheeses into clean, dry TM bowl and mill **8 sec/speed 8**. Remove from bowl and set aside.

2. Place remaining béchamel ingredients into TM bowl and cook **8 min/80°C/speed 4**.

3. Add approx. half the grated cheese and cook **2 min/90°C/speed 4**.

Assembly

1. In large rectangular baking dish, spread some ragu until the base of the dish is covered.

2. Top with lasagne sheets, béchamel, more ragu, lasagne sheets, béchamel and ragu finishing with lasagne and béchamel. You should have around 3–4 repeated layers.

3. Top béchamel with remaining grated cheese and bake covered with foil for 1 hour. Remove foil and brown top by increasing oven temperature to 180–200°C and cooking for a further 10–15 minutes.

4. Slice and serve hot with salad.

To roast a capsicum, place directly over a gas flame and turn with a long pair of tongs as each side becomes charred. This should take around 15–20 minutes. Remove from the flame and place into a glass bowl, cover with plastic wrap and allow to sweat until cool. Rub charred skin off flesh with a paper towel. Do not rinse the roasted capsicum as you will rinse off all the flavour.

THREE CHEESE AND MUSHROOM CALZONE

SERVES 8–10

NEED

- 1 batch Pizza Dough (see page 52)
- 100g Swiss or Dutch cheese, cubed
- 100g parmesan, cubed
- 3 cloves garlic

- 1 tsp fennel seeds
- 450g mushrooms, sliced
- 20g EVOO
- Handful basil leaves
- 2 handfuls baby spinach leaves

- 1 red capsicum, roasted and skinned, cut into strips
- 500g ricotta cheese

DO

1. Make dough and set aside.

2. Preheat pizza stone in 220°C oven on a bread setting if available.

3. Place Swiss and parmesan cheese into TM bowl and mill **10 sec/speed 8**. Remove from bowl and set aside.

4. Place garlic, and fennel into TM bowl and chop **3 sec/speed 7**.

5. Add mushrooms and EVOO and cook **5 min/Varoma/Reverse + speed 1** with MC off.

6. Add basil and spinach and cook **5 min/Varoma/Reverse + speed 1** with MC off. Drain any liquid and allow to cool slightly before assembly.

To assemble Calzone

1. Divide dough in half. For the base, roll half the dough into large circle on a piece of baking paper. Sprinkle with a little grated cheese and arrange half the red capsicum over. Spread with half the ricotta, and then top with all of the mushroom mixture. Repeat with grated cheese, and the remaining capsicum.

2. Roll other half of dough into a large circle and lay over the top of the pizza. Bring base dough up and over the top dough and pinch all the way around to seal edges.

3. Slide onto pizza stone and cook for approx. 25–30 minutes until golden all over.

4. Slice into large wedges and serve immediately.

TASTE

- Of course you can fill your calzone with any favourite pizza toppings. Feel free to add pestos, other cheeses, roasted vegies such as eggplant, pumpkin or zucchini, or meats as desired.

TOMATO TART TATIN

SERVES 8–10

Of course all the work in this is the homemade butter pastry. Rather than buy the commercial variety for this recipe I challenge you to make it yourself. This recipe is perfect for Sunday brunch but is so impressive, easy, and TO. DIE. FOR. that you will be trotting it out on special occasions just to see the looks on your guests' faces when they take a bite. But choose a day when the kids aren't home, when you can play some quiet zen music and channel your inner Tenina. It's not hard, but requires quiet time…if you can manage any of that.

NEED

- 1 batch Flaky Butter Pastry (see page 54)
- Few fresh basil leaves
- 3–4 cloves garlic, roughly chopped
- 500g cherry tomatoes (2 punnets)
- Pinch sea salt
- Pinch raw sugar
- Drizzle EVOO
- Balsamic vinegar to taste

DO

1. Preheat oven to 220°C.

2. Place a few basil leaves top side down into a flan tin with removable base.

3. Add chopped garlic, tomatoes and sprinkle with salt and sugar. Drizzle with EVOO and balsamic vinegar.

4. Roll pastry to fit the flan tin, tucking in all edges so that the tomato topping will not escape!

5. Bake 40–45 minutes until pastry is puffed and golden…maybe even a little darker than golden as you really want all the crispy layers happening.

6. Allow to cool slightly after removing from the oven, but not long enough to go soggy. Turn upside down onto serving dish and throw on a few more fresh basil leaves. Serve in large wedges whilst still hot, with a fresh garden salad.

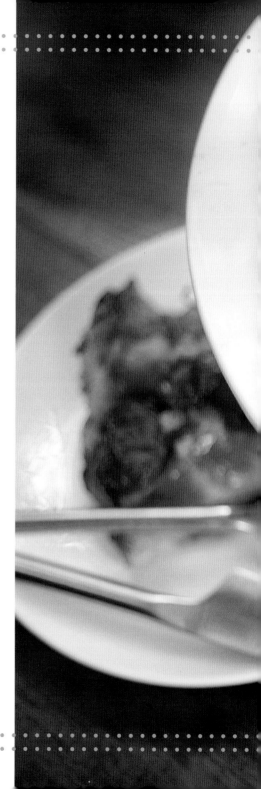

CORNED BEEF WITH THE TRIMMINGS

SERVES 8–10

I have to say that this is less a recipe and again, more of a suggestion. Of course the Parsley Sauce is science….
but the whole idea of corned beef in the TM just makes flavour sense. I hope you try it. If you feel that you
need a larger piece of beef, try cooking it in the steamer dish itself. It works. End. Of. Story.

NEED

- 1 onion, quartered
- 1 clove garlic
- 1 carrot, cut in pieces
- 1 stalk celery, cut in pieces
- 20g EVOO
- 3 cloves
- 2 bay leaves

- 1–2 sprigs fresh thyme
- Few peppercorns
- 30g malt vinegar
- 20g brown sugar
- 50g Umami Paste (see page 9)
- 1kg piece corned silverside (approx.)

- 1L water
- Carrots, beans, baby potatoes, etc.

DO

1. Place onion, garlic, carrot, celery and EVOO into TM bowl and chop **5 sec/speed 4**. Scrape down sides of bowl and sauté **5 min/Varoma/speed 1**.

2. Add cloves, bay leaves, thyme, peppercorns, vinegar, sugar and Umami Paste into TM bowl and meat into simmering basket. Insert basket into bowl.

3. Fill with water, but the amount may vary depending on the size of the meat you use. It should come up around the bottom of the meat and be visible.

4. Cook **60 min/90°C/speed 3**.

5. Place vegetables of choice into steamer dish and tray and set into position.

6. Cook **20 min/Varoma/speed 3**. If you are cooking green beans, only add them in the last 5 minutes.

7. Remove all food from the bowl and keep hot. Strain and reserve cooking liquid for Parsley Sauce (see across).

8. Slice meat, serve with vegetables and Parsley Sauce whilst hot.

PARSLEY SAUCE

=== **NEED** ===

- Handful Italian parsley
- 50g unsalted butter, cubed
- 25g flour
- 300g reserved cooking liquid
- 120g cream
- 2 tbsp seeded mustard
- Freshly ground black pepper to taste

=== **DO** ===

1. Place parsley into clean, dry TM bowl and chop **5 sec/ speed 7**. Remove from bowl and set aside.

2. Place butter and flour into TM bowl and chop **4 sec/ speed 5**.

3. Cook **5 min/Varoma/speed 2**.

4. Add 300g cooking liquid and cook **8 min/100°C/ speed 3**.

5. Add cream, mustard, chopped parsley and pepper and cook **2 min/100°C/speed 3**.

=== **TIP** ===

- If you want a pretty sauce, omit cooking liquid from recipe and replace with milk. Don't forget to season to taste.

LOST IN THE DESSERTS

I have always had a sweet tooth, and yet I found this chapter the hardest to write! My theory is that it was choosing the absolute cream of the crop that was the challenge. These desserts are all fantastic, and while some are easier than others, all are certainly worth the effort.
I have had advice from some real culinistas of the dessert world and there is one special treat that you should all attempt at least once. (Go Adriano Zumbo!)

CHOC CHERRY BRIOCHE PUDDING

SERVES 4–6

I was never a fan of the bread-and-butter pudding I grew up with, but get between me and my Choc Cherry Brioche Pudding and someone may get hurt. Amazing.

NEED

- ½ quantity Chocolate Cherry Brioche loaf (see page 47)
- 100g dried cherries
- 60g sugar
- 4 eggs + 2 egg yolks
- 150g cream
- 200g milk
- 60g brandy
- 1 tsp vanilla bean paste

DO

1. Preheat oven to 160°C. Butter 5–6 small ovenproof ceramic dishes.

2. Cube loaf and divide between prepared dishes.

3. Sprinkle cherries over.

4. Place sugar into TM bowl and mill **10 sec/speed 10**.

5. Add remaining ingredients and blend **15 sec/speed 6**. Pour over brioche.

6. Cook for 20–30 minutes until custard is set in centre.

7. Serve hot with ice-cream, or cream.

I love shortbread at Christmas,
but any time of the year is
great for these little bites. Just
a mouthful of crunch with a
hint of whatever sugar flavour
you choose. Subtle and somehow
evocative of your favourite
sidewalk café in Paris...well, of
mine anyway!

SCENTED SHORTBREAD

30–40 PIECES

NEED

- 120g flavoured sugar of choice (see across)
- 200g unsalted butter, cubed
- 320g plain flour
- 1 tsp vanilla bean paste
- Pinch coarse sea salt

DO

1. Preheat oven to fan-forced 180°C and line a baking tray with paper.

2. Place butter and 100g of the sugar in TM bowl and chop **4 sec/speed 6**.

3. Add flour, vanilla bean paste and salt and blend **10 sec/speed 6**. Tip dough out onto floured Silpat mat.

4. Divide into two or three portions. Roll each into a long sausage shape 3–4cm in diameter.

5. Roll in remaining flavoured sugar. Cut into small rounds, place onto tray and flatten with your thumb.

6. Bake for 12–15 minutes until golden and fragrant.

7. Cool before keeping in an airtight container in fridge for optimum crunch!

8. If you would like fresh shortbread at a moment's notice, don't cook it all at once, simply wrap one or two rolls of dough in baking paper and freeze until needed. Thaw slightly, slice and proceed with baking as directed.

FLAVOURED SUGARS

NEED

Rosemary Lemon Sugar
- Sprig rosemary, leaves only
- 140g raw sugar
- Zest 1 lemon

Orange Sugar
- 140g raw sugar
- Zest 1 orange

Cardamom Lemon Sugar
- 140g raw sugar
- 1 tsp cardamom seeds
- Zest 1 lemon

Lime Sugar
- 140g sugar
- Zest 2 limes

Crio Brü Chocolate Sugar
- 140g sugar
- 30g Crio Brü granules

DO

1. Place sugar and other ingredients into TM bowl and mill **10 sec/speed 10**. Use as needed in shortbread and reserve the rest.

MAPLE CHOCOLATE FUDGE

20-26 PIECES

I think I was born with a sweet tooth. Apparently if I went missing at the store, my mother would simply pick up a roll of Lifesavers and I would materialise as if by magic. Nothing has changed. I can smell chocolate at 10 paces and should you want my attention, present me with something sweet and I am all yours. (In a good way!) Fudge is the sweetest thing around, right in line before maple syrup and chocolate, so combine the three and you have a treat that is all sweet!
Disclaimer: Eat sparingly and with caution. Highly addictive.

NEED

- 500g sugar
- 400ml tin condensed milk
- Good pinch sea salt
- 65g maple syrup
- 100g unsalted butter, cubed
- 150g dark chocolate, in pieces

- 1 tsp vanilla bean paste
- Edible gold leaf (optional)

DO

① Place sugar into TM bowl and mill **40 sec/speed 10**.

② Add milk, salt, maple syrup and butter and cook **10 min/70°C/speed 3**.

③ Add chocolate and cook **15 min/100°C/speed 3**.

④ Remove MC and cook **35 min/Varoma/speed 2** using simmering basket on the lid to prevent spattering and help with reduction.

⑤ Add vanilla bean paste and blend **4 min/speed 7** with basket in place on lid. Scrape into a buttered 18cm square tin and allow to cool completely before refrigerating for up to 2 hours prior to cutting and serving.

If you want to elevate this to gift status, cut the pieces of fudge quite large. Push one piece onto the gold leaf, then use that piece as a tool to dab the other pieces. The gold leaf will stick to whatever it touches, including fingers, so be very careful. You need only 1-2 sheets. Gold leaf is available at specialist cake decorating stores.

SALTED CARAMEL AND MACADAMIA BROWNIES

12 BROWNIES

This recipe was the most visited post on my blog in 2010 so it had to be included here. I just love this recipe – the brownie is still gooey in the centre and the fragrance that fills your kitchen is amazing. It will make you feel all homey and gooey in the centre yourself!

= NEED =

- 300g dark brown sugar
- 90g unsalted butter, cubed
- 1 tsp vanilla bean paste
- 2 tsp sea salt, plus extra for topping
- 4 large eggs

- 1 large egg yolk
- 60g cacao powder
- 150g plain flour
- 100g macadamias
- 100g pecan or pistachio kernels

- Extra nuts and coarse sea salt for topping

= DO =

1. Preheat oven to fan-forced 180°C and line a 22cm square cake tin with baking paper that comes up over the edges for easy removal.

2. Place sugar, butter and vanilla into TM bowl and chop **5 sec/speed 6**. Cook **15 min/Varoma/speed 2**.

3. Add salt and incorporate **10 sec/speed 4**.

4. Add eggs, egg yolk and cacao powder to TM bowl and mix **15 sec/speed 5**.

5. Scrape down sides of bowl and add plain flour and nuts and mix **3 sec/speed 5**.

6. Spread into prepared pan, stud with additional nuts, sprinkle generously with sea salt and bake for 10 minutes.

7. Remove from oven and bang on bench quite firmly to prevent rise from continuing. Return to oven for a further 10 minutes or until just wobbly in centre.

8. Allow to cool slightly in tin before cutting into enormous pieces and wolfing down immediately!

RICH CHOCOLATE AND CRIO BRÜ BROWNIES

12-14 BROWNIES

I am going to say it in capitals – THESE ARE AMAZING. You will never go back to pedestrian old brownies. The texture improves the day after baking, but don't bet on them lasting that long. The addition of the Crio Brü, my favourite healthy chocolate product ever, adds that certain je ne sais quoi that makes you have to have another taste. You can, of course, add coffee granules or brewed coffee in the place of Crio Brü which is available online at http://criobru.com.au or ask for it at wholefood or specialty grocers. Don't scrimp on your cocoa either.

NEED

- 350g raw sugar
- 20g Crio Brü granules
- 40g cocoa
- Pinch sea salt
- 1 tsp vanilla bean paste
- 200g unsalted butter, cubed

- 250g plain flour
- 3 eggs
- 85g pecans kernels

Ganache
- 140g brewed Crio Brü liquid, hot
- 250g dark chocolate, in pieces

- Candied orange zest strips or additional Crio Brü granules to garnish

---
DO
---

① Preheat oven to 180°C and line a 30 x 20cm baking tin with paper and set aside.

② Place sugar and Crio Brü granules into TM bowl and mill **10 sec/speed 10**.

③ Add cocoa, salt, vanilla and butter and cook **5 min/80°C/speed 2**. (This mixture will be grainy.)

④ Add flour and eggs and blend **20 sec/speed 6**. Scrape down sides of bowl, add pecans and blend a further **4 sec/speed 5**.

⑤ Scrape into prepared tin and bake for 20 minutes or until inserted skewer comes out just a little sticky.

⑥ Meanwhile, make the ganache by placing Crio Brü and chocolate into clean TM bowl. Melt **1 min/50°C/ speed 2**. Scrape out of TM bowl and into a ceramic or glass bowl to cool completely before spreading onto Crio Brü Brownies.

⑦ Garnish with a few candied orange zest strips or dust with Crio Brü granules to taste.

You can never have too much energy, unless you are a two-year-old. So if you find yourself lagging, or, heaven forbid, feeling your age, whip up a batch of these and you'll be giving any two-year-old a run for their money. They're certainly working for me....

CHOCOLATE ENERGY BARS

16 BARS

NEED

- 300g blanched almonds, toasted
- 80g linseed
- Zest 1 orange
- ½ cinnamon stick
- 35g coconut, shredded
- Pinch sea salt

- 3 tbsp honey or pure maple syrup
- 2 tbsp Maca powder
- 3 tbsp coconut oil
- 50g Crio Brü grounds
- 1 tsp vanilla bean paste

Ganache
- 140g brewed Crio Brü liquid, hot
- 250g dark chocolate, in pieces

DO

1. Place ½ the almonds, linseed, orange zest and cinnamon stick into TM bowl and mill **10 sec/speed 8**.

2. Add remaining ingredients except remaining almonds and blend **20 sec/speed 8**.

3. Add almonds and blend **4 sec/speed 5**.

4. Press into lined rectangular baking tin and refrigerate for 30 minutes.

5. Meanwhile, make the ganache by placing strained Crio Brü liquid and chocolate into clean TM bowl. Melt together **1 min/50°C/speed 2**. Scrape out of TM bowl and into a ceramic or glass bowl to cool completely before spreading onto bars.

6. Cut into bars using sharp knife. Wrap separately and store in freezer until use.

TASTE

- These are a fantastic replacement for breakfast when on the run. Grab one and go. They can also be a wonderful pick-me-up in the afternoon at chocolate o'clock and a nutritious after-school snack.
- In the absence of Crio Brü, replace with coffee granules/liquid as written, but the results will not only taste different, but energy levels will peak and then drop as with all caffeine-related consumption.

CHOCOLATE COCONUT PIE

SERVES 12–16

This is without a doubt the best dessert recipe I have ever made. That's not to say I won't be coming up with something better in the future, but if I want to make an impression, flavour and texture-wise, this is it. Creamy, chocolatey, nutty, in short – divine. No more to say except fire up your TM and get cooking. You'll be just as impressive yourself.

NEED

Crust
- 130g unsalted butter, cubed
- Zest 1 lemon, finely grated
- 50g dark brown sugar
- 1 tsp vanilla extract
- 160g plain flour
- 1 pinch sea salt
- 50g each macadamias, pistachios and cashews

Filling
- 100g dark chocolate, in pieces
- 40g cocoa
- 400ml tin coconut cream
- 400ml tin coconut milk
- 100g sugar
- 1 tsp sea salt
- 2 tsp vanilla extract
- 80g corn flour

- 400–500g cream
- Chopped salted nuts or chocolate curls to garnish

DO

Crust

1. Preheat oven to 180°C on a fan-forced setting.

2. Place butter, zest and sugar into TM bowl and melt **4 min/37°C/speed 2**.

3. Add remaining crust ingredients and blend **15 sec/speed 6**.

4. Press into deep-sided flan tin with removable base (23cm diameter). Bake for 18 minutes or until golden and fragrant.

5. Cool completely before pouring in filling.

Filling

1. Place chocolate into TM bowl and mill **8 sec/ speed 8**.

2. Add cocoa, coconut cream and milk, sugar, salt, vanilla and corn flour. Cook **8 min/90°C/speed 4**.

3. Cook **3 min/100°C/speed 3**. Cool slightly before pouring into baked flan shell.

4. Press a piece of baking paper onto the surface of the filling to completely eliminate any air pockets. Keep in fridge until ready to serve.

5. Pour cream into TM bowl, insert Butterfly and whip **20–30 sec/speed 4** or until soft peaks form. Spread on top of pie, garnish with a few chocolate curls and additional nuts to taste.

WHITE CHOCOLATE CHEESECAKE WITH RASPBERRY GANACHE

SERVES 10–12

I should call this recipe 'Impress without Stress'. If you are searching for THE most impressive dessert, your search ends here. Who would have thought you could steam a cheesecake? Any baked cheesecake could probably benefit from a steamy environment, as it helps the texture, which can be dry. But be warned, there is no going back from here. Your cheesecake expectations will be forever different.

NEED

- 200g chocolate cream-filled biscuits (Oreos)
- 40g unsalted butter, cubed
- 400g white chocolate, in pieces
- 500g cream cheese
- 50g caster sugar
- 1 tsp vanilla bean paste

- 4 eggs

Ganache
- 20g good quality raspberry jam, (pushed through sieve to remove seeds)
- 100g dark chocolate, in pieces

- 50g cream
- Fresh or frozen raspberries to garnish

DO

1. Preheat oven to 180°C and line base of a 16cm springform cake tin with paper.

2. Place biscuits and butter into TM bowl and mill **15 sec/speed 6**.

3. Press into prepared tin and bake for 10 minutes. Remove from oven and cool.

4. Place white chocolate into TM bowl and chop **6 sec/speed 8**.

5. Scrape down sides of bowl and melt **10 min/50°C/speed 1**.

6. Add cream cheese, sugar, vanilla bean paste and eggs. Beat **1 min/speed 6**. Scrape down sides of bowl and repeat. Pour onto biscuit base.

7. Place cake tin on top of a pair of chopsticks in the steamer dish. (Chopsticks will help the steam circulate.)

8. Rinse bowl and fill with water to 1L mark. Set steamer into position

9. Cook cheesecake **60 min/Varoma/speed 3**. Chill until completely set in the centre. It will be slightly wobbly until cold.

Ganache

1. Place jam, dark chocolate and cream into TM bowl and melt **5 min/50°C/speed 1**. Place raspberries on top of ganache to decorate. Serve with additional whipped cream if desired.

This is a truly decadent dessert for a special occasion. Dacquoise is a nut meringue and I have developed the easiest method possible for the TM. It will be a flat, goopy, spreading mess when it goes into the oven, but you will be pleasantly surprised at the result and the taste is out of this world

Crio Beans are roasted cacao beans that have been dipped in a dairy-free chocolate. Available online at www.criobru.com.au

PECAN DACQUOISE WITH ORANGE CHOCOLATE CREAM

SERVES 10–12

NEED

- 1 roasted vanilla bean
- 300g pecans
- 300g sugar
- Zest 1 orange
- 6 egg whites
- 2 tbsp corn flour

Filling
- 45g chocolate Crio Beans + some more for garnish
- 600g whipping cream
- 2 tbsp cocoa

- 50g orange chocolate, in pieces
- 1 tsp unsalted butter

DO

1. Toast vanilla bean and pecans on flat oven tray for 10 minutes by placing into a cold oven set to 200°C. Set aside to cool. Reduce oven temperature to 160°C.

2. Draw an 18cm circle onto two sheets of baking paper and place onto flat trays. Set aside.

3. Place vanilla bean into TM bowl with 40g of the sugar and mill **10 sec/speed 10**. Remove from bowl and set aside.

4. Place cooled nuts into TM bowl and mill **8 sec/speed 8**. Remove from bowl and set aside. Wipe TM bowl.

5. Place sugar and zest into TM bowl and mill **30 sec/speed 9**. Reserve 2 tbsp sugar for cream filling.

6. Insert Butterfly. Add egg whites, corn flour and remaining vanilla sugar into TM bowl and beat **6 min/60°C/speed 3**.

7. Remove Butterfly. Add milled nuts to TM bowl and incorporate **15 sec/Interval**. Finish folding through by hand with spatula, if necessary. Divide mixture between circles on trays.

8. Bake for 40 mins. Remove from oven, cool slightly before lifting off paper with a large flat spatula. Cool completely on wire rack.

9. In clean, dry TM bowl place Crio Beans and chop **3 sec/speed 6**. Add reserved sugar, cream and cocoa. Insert Butterfly and whip cream till soft peaks form **20–30 sec/speed 4**. Top both dacquoise layers with this cream bringing it almost to the edges. Do not completely scrape out TM bowl – in fact leave quite a lot of the cream in the bowl. Scrape all of it down so that it is around the blades.

10. Place chocolate and butter into the bowl and melt **5 min/50°C/speed 2**. Drizzle over both layers, place one layer on top of the other. Garnish with additional Crio Beans or toasted pecans.

LIME MOUSSE PIE

SERVES 10–12

I don't often use ready-made ingredients, but I had some in my fridge on the day I came up with this recipe and the result was so good, they stayed. You can replace the vanilla yoghurt with plain yoghurt, but you may have to add sugar to taste and of course, the obligatory additional dash of vanilla bean paste.

NEED

- 350g butter shortbread (Walkers is recommended)
- 40g macadamia nuts, salted and roasted
- 15g gelatine granules
- Enough boiling water to cover (approx. 50g)
- Zest 2 limes, finely grated
- 50g sugar
- 90g lime juice, fresh
- 400g vanilla yoghurt
- 1 tsp vanilla bean paste
- 600ml cream
- Additional lime slices for garnish

DO

1. Preheat oven to 180°C. Butter a 23cm pie plate.
2. Place biscuits and nuts into TM bowl and mill **20 sec/speed 7** until a paste consistency is formed.
3. Press into pie plate and bake for 15 minutes. Cool.
4. Place gelatin into a bowl with enough boiling water to cover.
5. Place zest and sugar into TM bowl and mill **10 sec/speed 10**. Add juice, yoghurt and vanilla and blend **5 sec/speed 5**. Scrape down sides of bowl. Add gelatin to TM bowl and blend **20 sec/speed 6**. Remove from bowl and set aside.
6. Insert Butterfly and place cream into bowl. Whip **20–30 sec/speed 4** until very soft peaks form. Remove Butterfly.
7. Add lime mixture to cream and blend **10 sec/speed 7**.
8. Pour into cold biscuit base and allow to set for at least 4 hours. Garnish with lime slices and serve.

RASPBERRY AND ALMOND MERINGUE CAKE

SERVES 10–12

NEED

Cake
- 200g raw sugar
- 50g almonds
- 200g unsalted butter, cubed
- 2 eggs + 2 egg yolks
- 50g milk
- 1 tsp vanilla bean paste

- 220g self raising flour
- 100g raspberries

Meringue
- 100g raw sugar
- 3 egg whites
- Pinch cream of tartar
- 40g almond flakes

Filling
- 300g cream
- 40g Berry Lime Coulis (see page 17)
- Additional raspberries for garnish

DO

① Preheat oven to 160°C and line the base of 2 x 18cm non-stick cake tins with baking paper. Set aside.

② Place sugar and almonds into TM bowl and mill **10 sec/speed 10**.

③ Add butter, eggs, egg yolks, milk and vanilla bean paste and mix **10 sec/speed 7**. Add flour and blend **10 sec/speed 7**.

④ Add raspberries and stir through by hand, using a spatula. Divide between cake tins and spread to level.

⑤ To make meringue, place sugar into clean, dry TM bowl and mill **30 sec/speed 10**.

⑥ Insert Butterfly and add egg whites and cream of tartar. Whip **6 min/60°C/speed 3**.

⑦ Spread onto one of the cakes. Sprinkle with almond flakes.

⑧ Place cakes into oven and cook for 40–50 minutes. Remove cake without the meringue and cook other cake a further 20 minutes. Test cakes with a skewer to make sure they are cooked. Remove from oven and cool completely.

⑨ Place cream into TM bowl and insert Butterfly. Whip **20–30 sec/speed 4** or until soft peaks form. Add Berry Lime Coulis and stir through **4 sec/speed 1** for a mottled effect.

⑩ Place cake without meringue onto serving plate and top with cream. Add a few raspberries. Top with meringue cake layer and garnish with a few more raspberries and coulis. Serve.

This is my 'celebration' cake. It is so pretty and impressive without any real challenge in making it. It is a sure-fire winner every time, so don't be too distracted by the gorgeousness of it all. Just go ahead and try it. You won't be disappointed.

It is not often you see EVOO in a dessert, at least that you know of. I have used it in an eggless chocolate mousse, and it is fantastic. Look for a label that specifies that it is fruity...a lot like me really!

EVOO LEMON TART

SERVES 10–12

NEED

Crust
- 40g almonds, toasted and cooled
- 50g sugar
- 120g plain flour
- Pinch salt
- 80g unsalted butter, cubed
- 20g fruity EVOO
- 1 tsp vanilla bean paste
- 1 egg yolk

Filling
- Juice and zest 3 large lemons (at least 120g juice)
- 170g sugar
- 2 tbsp corn flour
- 2 eggs
- 2 egg yolks

- 75g unsalted butter, cubed
- 25g fruity EVOO

DO

1. To make crust, place almonds and sugar into TM bowl and mill **10 sec/speed 9**.

2. Add flour, salt and butter and blend **2 sec/speed 8**.

3. Add EVOO, vanilla bean paste and egg yolk and mix **10 sec/Interva**l so that it barely forms soft dough.

4. Press into 20cm flan dish with removable base and place in freezer for approx. 30 minutes.

5. Preheat oven to fan-forced 190°C. Bake pie shell for 13 minutes or until golden brown. Cool completely before filling.

6. To make filling, place zest and sugar into clean, dry TM bowl and mill **10 sec/speed 10**. Add juice, corn flour, eggs and egg yolks and blend **5 sec/speed 5**.

7. Insert Butterfly and cook **8 min/80°C/speed 3**. Remove Butterfly.

8. Add butter and EVOO and mix **20 sec/speed 5**. Scrape down sides of bowl and lid and repeat. Pour into cold pastry base and chill for several hours before serving in thin wedges.

BROWNED BUTTER CHERRY TART

SERVES 10–12

NEED

Pastry
- 70g sugar
- 1 strip lemon zest
- 90g unsalted butter, cubed
- 1 tsp vanilla bean paste
- 240g plain flour

Filling
- 100g caster sugar
- 2 eggs
- 70g unsalted butter, cubed
- 30g flour
- Pinch sea salt
- 2 tsp vanilla extract

- 680g jar Morello cherries drained or equivalent fresh, pitted

DO

1. Preheat oven to fan-forced 180°C and butter a flan tin with removable base.

2. Place sugar and lemon zest into TM bowl and mill **20 sec/speed 10**. Scrape down sides of bowl, add butter and melt **4 min/60°C/speed 2**. Cool slightly.

3. Add vanilla bean paste and flour and knead **20 sec/Interval** until mix resembles wet crumbs.

4. Press into flan tin and bake for 15 minutes or until golden and puffed up. Cool.

5. Without cleaning TM bowl, insert Butterfly, add sugar and eggs and beat **4 min/37°C/speed 3**.

6. Meanwhile, brown butter in a light-coloured saucepan on medium heat (Induction 5–6) stirring occasionally until it turns a nutty brown colour.

7. Do not over brown, err on the side of not brown enough. It will smell very fragrant and delicious, without any overtones of burnt! Set aside.

8. Complete the filling mixture by adding flour, salt and vanilla extract to TM bowl and mix **10 sec/speed 3**. Remove Butterfly before adding browned butter through hole in lid **30 sec/speed 3–4**.

9. Sprinkle cooked and cooled pastry base with cherries, spread filling topping over, using spatula to even out if necessary and then bake for further 20–25 minutes until puffed and golden.

10. Serve cold for best presentation.

If you hadn't noticed, I have a penchant for butter, and all the better if it has been browned. Beurre Noisette is fabulous in most things but I particularly love it with salt and crispy sage leaves on pasta or gnocchi. Here, it has been added to the topping of the tart. Once you taste it you will fall in love with nut brown butter, too.

RHUBERRY AND PISTACHIO CRUMBLE

SERVES 12

Please don't ask me where to get rhuberries …keep reading, keep reading. A combo made in a registry office, rhubarb and strawberries are so divine in the same mouthful that I keep repeating the match over and over again, and this recipe is no exception. Pistachios are also one of my faves and here they are again as well. And what's not to love about cardamom? This is a perfect winter dessert, but who is looking to see what the weather is going to be?

═══ NEED ═══

Filling
- 30g Cardamom Lemon Sugar (see page 121)
- 300g rhubarb, chopped
- 1 green apple, peeled and cubed
- Zest 1 orange, finely grated
- 50g orange juice, fresh
- 300g strawberries

Crumble
- 65g Cardamom Lemon Sugar (see page 121)
- pinch sea salt
- 100g butter, cubed
- 1 tsp vanilla bean paste
- 70g plain flour

- 120g rolled oats
- 100g pistachios, shelled

═══ DO ═══

Filling

1. Place Cardamom Lemon Sugar, rhubarb, apple, zest and juice into TM bowl and cook **8 min/100°C/Reverse + speed 1**.

2. Pour into ovenproof dish (or individual dishes) and top evenly with sliced strawberries.

3. Preheat oven to 170°C.

Crumble

1. In clean, dry TM bowl, place Cardamom Lemon Sugar, salt and butter and mix **4 sec/speed 5**.

2. Add remaining ingredients except pistachios and blend **4 sec/Reverse + speed 5**. Add pistachios and blend **3 sec/Reverse + speed 5**.

3. Place crumble on top of filling, spreading to fill gaps. Bake for 40–50 minutes until golden and fragrant. A little of the filling juice should burst through the crumble and caramelise.

4. Serve piping hot with custard, cream, vanilla bean ice-cream, mascarpone or all of the above!

The Crio Brü granules will provide a little chocolate crunch to your cream if served immediately. They absorb moisture and so over time will soften and blend with the cream.

HAZELNUT MERINGUE WITH
CRIO BRÜ CREAM AND STRAWBERRIES

SERVES 10–12

This is yet another dessert of note. It is so pretty, with the chocolate and the strawberries, that I think it is wonderful at Christmas time. And at any other time, of course. Do not be dismayed if the meringue part looks a little flat on its way out of the oven. Mound up that to-die-for chocolate cream, add the berries and you will have an audience of willing admirers just drooling to be the first to dig in.

NEED

- 220g sugar
- 250g hazelnuts, roasted and skinned
- 130g egg whites (approx. 4 large)
- 1 pinch cream of tartar
- 1 tsp vanilla bean paste
- 400g cream
- 20g cocoa
- 1–2 tbsp Crio Brü granules
- 200–300g strawberries, sliced

DO

1. Preheat oven to 150°C and line a large flat tray with baking paper. Draw a 15cm circle onto the paper. Set aside.

2. Place sugar and hazelnuts into TM bowl and mill **10 sec/speed 9**. Remove from bowl and set aside in large mixing bowl. Clean and dry TM bowl.

3. Insert Butterfly and place egg whites and cream of tartar into TM bowl. Whip **6 min/60°C/speed 3**.

4. Add to sugar and nut mixture and fold through by hand using gentle folding motion, until well incorporated. The mixture will be quite sticky.

5. Scrape onto prepared tray, within the boundaries of the circle. The cake will spread when cooking.

6. Cook for 1 hour. Remove from oven and cool.

7. Insert Butterfly into clean TM bowl. Add vanilla bean paste, cream, cocoa and Crio Brü granules and whip **20–30 sec/speed 4** until soft peaks form.

8. Mound cream on top of meringue, leaving a 3cm circumference around edges without cream. Garnish with strawberries.

SPONGE ROLL WITH CARAMEL BUTTERCREAM FILLING

SERVES 6–8

NEED

- 50g corn flour
- 120g self raising flour
- 240g sugar
- 4 eggs, separated
- Pinch cream of tartar
- 1 tsp vanilla bean paste

- 1 batch Caramel Buttercream Filling (see across)
- A few raspberries or strawberries to taste
- Icing sugar

DO

1. Preheat oven to 170°C and line a Swiss roll tin with baking paper. Sprinkle with a little caster sugar and set aside.

2. Sift corn flour and flour together in TM bowl **10 sec/speed 7**. Remove from bowl and set aside on baking paper.

3. Place sugar into TM bowl and mill **10 sec/speed 10**. Remove from bowl and set aside. Clean bowl with dry paper towel.

4. Insert Butterfly. Place egg whites and cream of tartar into TM bowl and whip **4 min/60°C/speed 3**.

5. Add sugar 1 tsp at a time through hole in lid as you continue to whip **4 min/60°C/speed 3**. Remove from bowl and place meringue in a large mixing bowl.

6. Without cleaning bowl, and with Butterfly in position, add egg yolks and vanilla. Whip **4 min/60°C/speed 3**. Remove from bowl and add to whites.

7. Using large metal spoon, fold flour, whites and egg yolks together until you have a fluffy batter. Be as gentle as possible at this stage.

8. Spread onto prepared tray and bake for 20 minutes or until golden and springing back when touched.

9. Turn onto another piece of baking paper sprinkled with a little caster sugar. Peel the baking paper off. Roll while still warm, and place seam side down on baking tray to cool.

10. Unroll gently. It will not fully flatten, so do not force it. Spread with Caramel Buttercream Filling, sprinkle with a few berries of choice and re-roll. Refrigerate until frosting is firm. Dust with a little icing sugar, slice and serve.

This is the one recipe you really must be careful with. Add the sugar slowly, don't rush the folding in, don't hurry the rolling up of the cake once cooked. Treat it with care and it will look and taste amazing. Instead of serving with Caramel Buttercream, try Citrus Curd and whipped cream, or drizzle with Berry Lime Coulis, or the Ganache from the Rich Chocolate and Crio Brä Brownies or Pecan Dacquoise.

CARAMEL BUTTERCREAM FILLING
NEED

- 35g plain flour
- 200g whole milk
- 150g brown sugar

- 200g unsalted butter
- Pinch sea salt
- Dash of brandy

- 2 tsp vanilla bean paste

DO

❶ Place flour and milk into TM bowl and blend **5 sec/speed 6**. Cook **10 min/ 80°C/speed 4**. Pour into bowl, cover with plastic wrap, pushing plastic down onto surface of mixture. Cool completely.

❷ Place sugar, 30g of the butter, salt, brandy and vanilla and chop **5 sec/speed 7**. Cook **10 min/Varoma/speed 2**. Remove from bowl and cool completely.

❸ Place cooked milk paste, cold caramel and remaining butter into TM bowl and blend **6 sec/speed 6**.

❹ Insert Butterfly. Beat **1 min/speed 4** until very smooth. Cover and refrigerate for 15 minutes. Use immediately. This frosting cannot be made ahead of time, but you can make the roux and caramel ahead if you need to.

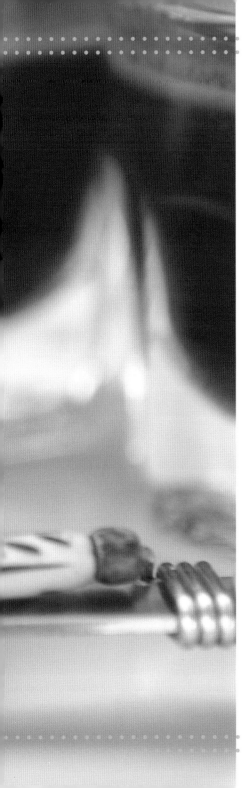

VANILLA THRILLER SLICE

20 PIECES

Do not be daunted by this cake. Try it once…before you know it you will be making it for every special occasion and will barely need to look at the recipes.

Vanilla Thriller Slice is a less challenging version of the very impressive Vanilla Thriller or V8 cake that became a star in its own right on the first season of MasterChef Australia. Designed by the talented Adriano Zumbo, I managed to make the original once with his constant tutelage over the phone. Believe me, it really was 'Phone a friend' time! Adriano kindly allowed me to play around with his recipe for this book and indeed, he is the inspiration behind this amazing, uniquely Aussie slice….this is like no school tuckshop Vanilla Slice you have ever eaten. Enjoy.

═══ TIP ═══

- On the following 3 pages you will find recipes for the 7 components of the Vanilla Thriller Slice and instructions on its assembly.
- The best tin you could use is a 22cm square cake tin with a removable base. It will make everything so much easier.
- Make the Dacquoise FIRST.
- Roast your vanilla beans and almonds for the entire recipe all in one hit in 200°C oven for 10 minutes, give the almonds a stir and maybe add 1–2 minutes if needed.
- The Vanilla Glaze is optional, but it certainly finishes Vanilla Thriller Slice off perfectly. The titanium dioxide is an edible white pigment used largely in the confectionery industry. It is what makes marshmallows white. It is available online from The Melbourne Food Ingredient Depot at www.mfcd.net

VANILLA ALMOND DACQUOISE

NEED

- 220g sugar
- 1 vanilla bean, roasted
- 250g blanched almonds, toasted
- 130g egg whites (4 large)
- Pinch cream of tartar

DO

1. Preheat oven to 150°C and line a flat tray with baking paper. Mark the paper in the shape and size of the tin you will be using for the entire slice. Set aside.

2. Place sugar, vanilla bean and almonds into TM bowl and mill **10 sec/speed 10**.

3. Remove from bowl and set aside in large mixing bowl. Clean and dry TM bowl.

4. Insert Butterfly and place egg whites and cream of tartar into TM bowl. Whip **6 min/60°C/speed 3**.

5. Add to sugar and nut mixture and fold through by hand using gentle folding motion, until well incorporated. The mixture will be quite sticky.

6. Scrape onto prepared tray, inside the boundaries of the marked paper. The cake will spread when cooking. Cook for 1 hour.

7. Remove from oven and cool, cut to the size of fit the base of your tin and press into the tin.

8. This layer can be made up to 2 days ahead.

VANILLA ALMOND CRUNCH

NEED

- 1 vanilla bean, roasted
- 50g milk or dark couverture chocolate, in pieces
- 100g Almond Praline Paste (see across)
- 100g Pure Almond Paste (see across)
- 20g blanched almonds, toasted, roughly chopped
- 20g unsalted butter
- 50g Brown Sugar Crumble (see across)
- 50g crunchy wheat flake cereal (Wheaties)
- Pinch sea salt
- 1 tsp vanilla bean paste

DO

1. Place vanilla bean with a little sugar into TM bowl and mill to a fine powder **10–15 sec/speed 8–9**. Set aside.

2. Place chocolate into TM bowl and mill **10 sec/speed 9**.

3. Melt **3 min/37°C/speed 1**.

4. Add Almond Praline Paste, Pure Almond Paste and toasted almonds and mix **5 sec/speed 5**.

5. Melt butter in shallow pan and bring to noisette (nut brown) stage. This is a delicate process. You want lots of tiny brown flecks in the butter, which is the caramelised milk solids, without burning them. It is easier to see the brown butter forming in a pan with a light-coloured base.

6. Add reserved vanilla bean powder, brown butter and remaining ingredients to TM bowl and mix **5 sec/ Reverse + speed 2**.

7. Press onto the Dacquoise layer and spread until even, with a silicone spatula. Refrigerate.

ALMOND PRALINE PASTE

NEED

- 100g sugar
- 100g blanched almonds, toasted
- 2 tbsp almond oil (if needed)

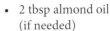

DO

1. Place sugar into shallow pan and on low to medium heat (Induction 4), cook without stirring until sugar melts and creates a liquid caramel. Pour onto Silpat mat and allow to cool until solid.

2. Break into pieces. Place toffee and almonds into TM bowl and mill **30 sec/speed 6–7** until oils are released from almonds and it starts to form a paste. Scrape down sides of bowl, add almond oil if needed and blend **10–15 sec/speed 6–7**. Set aside.

PURE ALMOND PASTE

NEED

- 100g blanched almonds, toasted
- 2–3 tsp almond oil

DO

1. Place cooled almonds and almond oil into TM bowl and mill **25–30 sec/speed 6** or until smooth paste is formed.

2. You may like to try adding the almond oil a little at a time, as some almonds are more oily than others, and some almonds may not need oil at all.

BROWN SUGAR CRUMBLE

NEED

- 50g blanched almonds, toasted
- ½ vanilla bean, roasted
- 50g unsalted butter
- 50g plain flour
- 50g dark brown sugar

DO

1. Place almonds and vanilla bean into TM bowl and mill **10 sec/speed 10**.

2. Add remaining ingredients and mix **10 sec/speed 7**.

3. To form crumble, press dough through a cooling rack with lined baking tray underneath.

4. Bake for 10–15 minutes in 180°C oven and allow to cool before adding to Vanilla Almond Crunch recipe.

TIP

- Leftovers from this part of the recipe are delicious and it would make a great cookie recipe all by itself.

VANILLA GANACHE

NEED

- 300g white chocolate, in pieces
- 1 vanilla bean, roasted
- 180g cream
- 1 tsp corn flour
- 1 tsp vanilla bean paste
- 100g unsalted butter, cubed

DO

1. Place chocolate and vanilla bean into TM bowl and mill **10 sec/speed 10**.

2. Add remaining ingredients and mix **2 min/speed 7–8** until thick creamy consistency is achieved. Remove from bowl and place into glass or ceramic bowl.

3. Spread on top of Vanilla Almond Crunch Layer and smooth with a wet spatula. Cover by pressing plastic wrap onto surface of ganache and keep in the fridge until you are ready to apply the glaze.

VANILLA GLAZE

NEED

- 200g cream
- 2 tsp vanilla sugar
- 1 x 12g sachet cake glaze (RUF brand, available at European specialty stores)
- 1 tsp titanium dioxide (optional, purely for the white look)

DO

1. Place all ingredients into TM bowl and blend **5 sec/speed 7**. Scrape down sides of bowl and cook **4 min/70°C/speed 3**.

2. Spread glaze on top of cold Vanilla Ganache. Work quickly as it will set fast.

TIP

- DO NOT make the glaze until the rest of the slice is assembled.

ASSEMBLY

DO

1. Cut the Vanilla Almond Dacquoise to fit the base of your tin and press into the tin.

2. Spread Vanilla Almond Crunch on top of Dacquoise in tin that has a removable base. Smooth with a wet silicone spatula to get an even surface. Refrigerate.

3. Spread Vanilla Ganache on top of Almond Crunch and smooth with a wet spatula. Cover with cling film, pushing it down onto the surface of the ganache.

4. Spread Vanilla Glaze on top of Vanilla Ganache. Allow to set completely before un-moulding.

5. Push out of tin and slice edges off with sharp knife that you clean between each cut. The flavour will improve over a few days. Serve in slivers with some fresh berries to cut through the sweetness.

RICH CHOCCIE ICE-CREAM

SERVES 10–12

Once you try this version of ice-cream you will never go back to the purchased variety without wistfully longing for a scoop of it. Imagine adding nuts, choc chips or chunks, toffee, caramel ribbons, berries or all of the above. Seriously good ice-cream, and all at the flick of a switch (or two).

NEED

- 200g dark chocolate, in pieces
- 3 eggs
- 170g caster sugar
- 350g cream
- 250g milk
- 1 tsp vanilla bean paste
- Pinch sea salt

DO

1. Place chocolate in TM bowl and chop **5 sec/speed 8**.

2. Remove from bowl and set aside.

3. Place eggs and sugar into TM bowl insert Butterfly. Beat **4 min/37°C/speed 3**.

4. Add remaining ingredients, including chopped chocolate. Cook **6 min/80°C/speed 3**.

5. Pour into large metal loaf tin. Cool.

6. Place in freezer for approx. 2 hours or until frozen around the edges.

7. Return to TM bowl and beat **30 sec/speed 9**.

8. Return to loaf pan and freeze overnight.

9. You can beat it again if you would like it to be a lighter mixture...but I personally like a 'heavy' ice-cream. It goes better with my hips.

10. Scoop into bowls or waffle cones.

TURKISH DELIGHT ICE-CREAM TORTE

12 INDIVIDUAL TORTES

I love this dessert on Christmas Day and have made it the past few years just for that occasion. It is so pretty and festive. So from me to you, Merry Christmas, unless of course you want to make it at Easter, in which case, Happy Easter.

NEED

- 1 recipe Berry Lime Coulis (see page 17)
- 230g butter shortbread biscuits (Walkers is recommended)
- 55g blanched almonds, toasted
- 55g sugar

- 2 eggs
- 300g chilled cream
- ½ tsp rosewater (optional)
- 50g craisins (dried cranberries)
- 50g pistachio kernels

- 100g each pink and green Turkish delight, cubed (available at specialty stores)

DO

1. Make Berry Lime Coulis and cool.

2. Pre-heat oven to fan-forced 180°C. Line base of a 13cm springform pan or for individual tortes, butter a muffin or friand tin and set aside.

3. Place shortbread biscuits and almonds into clean TM bowl and mill **10 sec/speed 10**.

4. Press into pan and bake for 10 minutes. Cool completely.

5. Place sugar into clean, dry TM bowl and mill **10 sec/speed 10**. Insert Butterfly.

6. Add eggs and cook **6 min/60°C/speed 3**. Pour into separate bowl and chill.

7. Pour cream and rosewater into TM bowl and whip **10–20 sec/speed 4** until soft peaks form. Fold by spatula into chilled custard and then fold through remaining ingredients except Berry Lime Coulis.

8. Pour into base and then pour coulis on top. Stir through with a skewer to create a marbled effect.

9. Freeze for 4 hours or more before serving. Garnish un-moulded torte with fresh berries, mint leaves and additional pistachios or Turkish delight pieces as desired, and dust with icing sugar.

10. To assist with serving, place in fridge 20 minutes before un-moulding and slicing.

CONTENTS

CATEGORY A-Z

Hub & Spoke Publishing®

Published by Hub & Spoke Publishing
4 Aberdeen Street
Perth, Western Australia 6000
www.hubandspoke.com.au

First published by Hub & Spoke Publishing, 2011
5th reprint, 2014

Design concept & art direction:
braincells Strategic Creative Marketing
Photography: Shea Walsh
Food Styling: Tenina Holder

The Publisher would like to thank the following organizations
and people for their assistance in the publication of this book:
braincells Strategic Creative Marketing, Darren Purchese, Pam
Casellas, Dr. Chris Davies, Lucille Fisher, Jennifer Goetz, Mandy
Marais, Kate Nelson, Nicolas Poelaert, Teller & Associates, Christa
Walsh, Shea Walsh and Adriano Zumbo.

National Library of Australia Cataloguing-in-Publication entry

Author:	Holder, Tenina.
Title:	For food's sake : recipes for use with a Thermomix / Tenina Holder.
ISBN:	9780987148926 (hbk.)
Notes:	Includes index.
Subjects:	Food processor cooking. Kitchen appliances. Cooking.

Dewey Number: 641.5892

Printed and bound in China by RR Donnelley Asia.

Hub & Spoke Publishing has no association with, sponsorship of, or licence from Vorwerk
International AG or Thermomix in Australia Pty Ltd. Any recipes used in this publication have
not been authorised, tested or approved by Vorwerk International AG or Thermomix in Australia
Pty Ltd. The Thermomix™ logo is a registered trade mark in Australia, owned by Vorwerk
International AG.